# Explore the Core

## FOURTH GRADE

Series Editor/Author
Janet Tassell

Assistant Editors/Authors of Authentic Challenge Projects
Marge Maxwell and Rebecca Stobaugh

Authors of Pre/Post Assessments and Problem Sets
Pamela Morris Jukes and Janet Cole

GARLIC PRESS
*Educational Materials for Teachers and Parents*

GARLIC PRESS

*Educational Materials for Teachers and Parents*

899 South College Mall Road
Bloomington, IN 47401

# www.garlicpress.com

Publisher: Douglas M. Rife
Authors: Pamela Morris Jukes and Janet Cole
Series Editor/Author: Janet Tassell
Assistant Editors/Authors of Authentic Challenge Projects:
Marge Maxwell and Rebecca Stobaugh
Authors of Pre/Post Assessments and Problem Sets:
Pamela Morris Jukes and Janet Cole
Reviewers: Megan Roper, Sara Prather, Ashley Hutsell
Art Director: Joanne Caroselli
Illustrators: Marilynn Barr, Joanne Caroselli, Sherry Neidigh, Michelle Ste. Marie
Interior Design: Joanne Caroselli
Cover Design: Jenn Taylor

ISBN: 978-1-930820-27-2

# Dear Teacher/Parent,

Mathematics can be one of the most exhilarating experiences a child has while imparting confidence and power to bolster all thinking in school and educational endeavors. Our hope with this unique book is to give the tools necessary to capture the wonder and fun with mathematics and help teachers and parents instruct the Common Core Mathematics Standards in a manageable way.

## THE COMMON CORE STANDARDS CONNECTION:

The focus of this book is to spotlight and connect to the Standards for Mathematical Content. However, throughout, we also want to turn an eye toward some of the key Standards for Mathematical Practice:

### Make sense of problems and persevere in solving them.

This text includes problems that are challenging and require more than a simple answer, where students explain their work and their thinking.

### Model with mathematics.

This book includes practice problems encompassing many real-world situations and the Authentic Challenge Problems pushing students to engage in everyday problems that involve mathematical reasoning.

### Use appropriate tools strategically.

The students are encouraged in the problem sets to use the tools necessary to solve problems for the scenarios given, such as rulers, calculators, etc. and even take it to the next level to analyze the outcome strategically.

## THE OVERALL DESIGN:
In a workbook design, we understood from the onset that it would not be possible in a succinct manner to be comprehensive in nature, but yet we did try to hit the high points of what we believed would be a best representation of the Standards in the following design:

- Self-Monitoring Chart
- Pre-Post Assessment for each Standard Domain
- Problem Sets for each Standard in each Standard Domain
- Authentic Challenge Projects
- Answer Key

**PROGRESS-MONITORING CHART:** The chart will allow the student the opportunity to chart success on the pre/post assessment and the problem sets so as to be accountable for his/her own learning and work toward personal goals and awareness of progress of their own understanding of the mathematics Standards.

**PRE-POST ASSESSMENT:** The pre/post assessments afford the student and the teacher the capability to pinpoint the students' strengths and concerns prior to going into the Standard section. This will allow a chance for self-monitoring where the student can keep track of his/her own individual progress. Each Standard Domain has a Pre/Post Assessment that is the same and only one copy at the beginning of the Standard section. (Remember to photocopy this before use if you plan to use this for a post-test!) On the Pre/Post Assessment, each Standard has at least two questions or answer parts. This is a snapshot for each Standard – not meant to be comprehensive but a brief picture of what the student knows to inform as for next steps. If the student answers all of the questions on the Standard section correctly on the pre-assessment, the decision may very likely be that the student does not do that corresponding Problem Set. However, if the student misses half or all of the questions on the pre-assessment for a Standard, the corresponding Problem Set would be highly suggested to help students enrich their conceptual understanding of that Standard.

**PROBLEM SETS:** Each Standard has a devoted Problem Set that has a minimum of 5 questions or answer parts. Our hope was to always, when possible, set the problems in a context that was challenging and authentic. We did not want this to be another book on the shelf that was retroactively stated as "aligned to the Common Core Standards" – we *Created* this and designed this book to be user-friendly and easy to implement in elementary mathematics instruction. We also designed rigorous problems that teachers tend to find difficult to write themselves or challenging to locate these types of problems. There are plenty of books on the market already with only rote memorization and low-level problems. Our book offers variety -- it is unique and different.

**AUTHENTIC CHALLENGE PROJECTS:** This section is a novel segment of the book where we have included authentic opportunities for the student to connect with the mathematics standards in an integrated way with other disciplines and technology. Our hope is that the student will see mathematics come alive through the authentic setting and be inspired to tackle the challenge as many of the projects are related to students' interests.

**ANSWER KEY:** Due to the ramped up rigor in the Common Core Standards, we decided to especially design this section to be detailed beyond the typical textbook answer keys. We are hopeful that students and others better learn about their answers and gain an understanding of how to work the problems when necessary.

# Self-Monitoring Chart

This chart is to aid in helping students in self-monitoring their progress toward growth in the Standards. The chart should be used to record scores on the pre-assessment for each standard section with the score of correct answers over the total possible. The next column is where the score for each problem set can be documented. It is then recommended that the student complete the post-assessment for the standards that were not mastered in the pre-assessment.

| Domain #1 OA | Pre-Assessment Score | Problem Set Score | Post-Assessment Score |
|---|---|---|---|
| 4.OA.A.1 | | | |
| 4.OA.A.2 | | | |
| 4.OA.A.3 | | | |
| 4.OA.B.4 | | | |
| 4.OA.C.5 | | | |
| Domain #2 NBT | Pre-Assessment Score | Problem Set Score | Post-Assessment Score |
| 4.NBT.A.1 | | | |
| 4.NBT.A.2 | | | |
| 4.NBT.A.3 | | | |
| 4.NBT.B.4 | | | |
| 4.NBT.B.5 | | | |
| 4.NBT.B.6 | | | |
| Domain #3 NF | Pre-Assessment Score | Problem Set Score | Post-Assessment Score |
| 4.NF.A.1 | | | |
| 4.NF.A.2 | | | |
| 4.NF.B.3 | | | |
| 4.NF.B.4 | | | |
| 4.NF.C.5 | | | |
| 4.NF.C.6 | | | |
| 4.NF.C.7 | | | |
| Domain #4 MD | Pre-Assessment Score | Problem Set Score | Post-Assessment Score |
| 4.MD.A.1 | | | |
| 4.MD.A.2 | | | |
| 4.MD.A.3 | | | |
| 4.MD.B.4 | | | |
| 4.MD.C.5 | | | |
| 4.MD.C.6 | | | |
| 4.MD.C.7 | | | |
| Domain #5 G | Pre-Assessment Score | Problem Set Score | Post-Assessment Score |
| 4.G.A.1 | | | |
| 4.G.A.2 | | | |
| 4.G.A.3 | | | |

# Meet the Writers

**Pamela Morris Jukes** received her doctorate in Curriculum and Instruction from the University of Kentucky and is currently serving as an Associate Professor in the School of Teacher Education at Western Kentucky University. She teaches both graduate and undergraduate courses in classroom management, teaching strategies, unit development, and teacher leadership. She serves on the Content Area Program Review Committee for the state of Kentucky and is a state trainer for the Kentucky Teacher Internship Program. She serves as Program Representative for the Elementary Education Program at WKU and works closely with local public schools in the under- graduate field-based program and as consultant. In addition, she supervises first year teachers during the intern process. Prior to her work at WKU she taught P-6 students for eleven years. She currently lives in Bowling Green, Kentucky with her husband, Jon, and their daughter, Hannah Margaret.

**Janet Cole** has been a fourth grade teacher in the Warren County Public Schools system in Kentucky for six years. She received her bachelor and master degrees from Western Kentucky University. Janet is a scholar of the Math and Technology Leadership Academy, a program funded by Toyota through Western Kentucky University to provide further education for teachers to instill higher level thinking skills in students. In her spare time, Janet enjoys camping and spending time with her husband Wade and their children Ryan, Kathryn, and Erin and participating in church activities.

# Meet the Editors

**Janet Tassell** began her career teaching mathematics then spent 14 years as Director of Learning and Assessment working with K-12 teachers in curriculum and professional development. During this time, she learned the importance of teachers needing rigorous materials aligned to the standards. She earned her Ph.D. from Indiana University in Curriculum and Instruction – mathematics and gifted education. She is now an Assistant Professor at Western Kentucky University, Bowling Green, Kentucky, where she teaches Elementary Math Methods and directs the Elementary Mathematics Specialist Endorsement program. She has been the co-director of the Toyota Math and Technology Leadership Academy and the professional development coordinator for the Javits grant Project GEMS (Gifted Education for Math and Science) initiative for grades 3-6 students. Recently, she and her husband, Brad, published a book connecting reading and mathematics fluency: *Speaking of Math – Fluency Poems for Partners: Addition.*

**Marge Maxwell** has been a teacher, school district supervisor, and university professor of educational technology. She was a special education teacher, supervisor of special education, and a supervisor of instructional technology before moving on to the university level. She earned her Ph.D. in Curriculum and Instruction with an emphasis in educational technology. Currently, she is an associate professor at Western Kentucky University in the Library Media Education master's degree program. Her research interests include effectiveness of online instruction; integrating critical thinking, authentic learning, and technology to produce deeper student learning; and connecting reform with Common Core Standards.

**Rebecca Stobaugh** has been a principal and middle and high school teacher. As a middle school and high school teacher, she was named Social Studies Teacher of the Year by the Kentucky Council for Social Studies in 2004. In her position as a middle school principal, she focused on aligning curriculum, increasing the level of critical thinking in assessments and instruction, and establishing a school-wide discipline plan. She is the author of two books: *Assessing Critical Thinking in Elementary Schools* and *Assessing Critical Thinking in Middle and High Schools.* She received a PhD from the University of Louisville. Currently, she serves as an assistant professor at Western Kentucky University, teaching assessment and unit-planning courses in the teacher education program. She supervises first-year teachers and consults with school districts on critical thinking, instructional strategies, assessment, technology integration, and other topics.

# Table of Contents

## DOMAIN 1: OPERATIONS & ALGEBRAIC THINKING

**4.OA.A.1.** Interpret a multiplication equation as a comparison.

**4.OA.A.2**. Multiply or divide to solve word problems involving multiplicative comparison.

**4.OA.A.3.** Solve multistep word problems posed with whole numbers and having whole-number answers using the four operations, including problems in which remainders must be interpreted.

**4.OA.B.4.** Find all factor pairs for a whole number in the range 1–100. Recognize that a whole number is a multiple of each of its factors. Determine whether a given whole number in the range 1–100 is a multiple of a given one-digit number. Determine whether a given whole number in the range 1–100 is prime or composite.

**4.OA.C.5.** Generate a number or shape pattern that follows a given rule. Identify apparent features of the pattern that were **NOT** explicit in the rule itself.

## DOMAIN 2: NUMBER & OPERATIONS IN BASE TEN

**4.NBT.A.1** Recognize that in a multi-digit whole number, a digit in one place represents ten times what it represents in the place to its right.(17)

**4.NBT.A.2.** Read and write multi-digit whole numbers using base-ten numerals, number names, and expanded form. Compare two multi-digit numbers based on meanings of the digits in each place, using >, =, and < symbols to record the results of comparisons.

**4.NBT.A.3.** Use place value understanding to round multi-digit whole numbers to any place.

**4.NBT.B.4.** Fluently add and subtract multi-digit whole numbers using the standard algorithm.

**4.NBT.B.5.** Multiply a whole number of up to four digits by a one-digit whole number, and multiply two two-digit numbers, using strategies based on place value and the properties of operations. Illustrate and explain the calculation by using equations, rectangular arrays, and/or area models.

**4.NBT.B.6.** Find whole-number quotients and remainders with up to four-digit dividends and one-digit divisors, using strategies based on place value, the properties of operations, and/or the relationship between multiplication and division. Illustrate and explain the calculation by using equations, rectangular arrays, and/or area models.

## DOMAIN 3: NUMBER & OPERATIONS—FRACTIONS

**4.NF.A.1.** Explain why a fraction $a/b$ is equivalent to a fraction $(n \times a)/(n \times b)$ by using visual fraction models, with attention to how the number and size of the parts differ even though the two fractions themselves are the same size. Use this principle to recognize and generate equivalent fractions.

**4.NF.A.2.** Compare two fractions with different numerators and different denominators, e.g., by creating common denominators or numerators, or by comparing to a benchmark fraction such as 1/2. Recognize that comparisons are valid only when the two fractions refer to the same whole. Record the results of comparisons with symbols >, =, or <, and justify the conclusions, e.g., by using a visual fraction model.

**4.NF.B.3.** Understand a fraction $a/b$ with $a > 1$ as a sum of fractions $1/b$.
a. Understand addition and subtraction of fractions as joining and separating parts referring to the same whole.
b. Decompose a fraction into a sum of fractions with the same denominator in more than one way, recording each decomposition by an equation.
c. Add and subtract mixed numbers with like denominators, e.g., by replacing each mixed number with an equivalent fraction, and/or by using properties of operations and the relationship between addition and subtraction.
d. Solve word problems involving addition and subtraction of fractions referring to the same whole and having like denominators, e.g., by using visual fraction models and equations to represent the problem.

**4.NF.B.4.** Apply and extend previous understandings of multiplication to multiply a fraction by a whole number.
a. Understand a fraction *a/b* as a multiple of 1/*b*. *For example, use a visual fraction model to represent 5/4 as the product 5 × (1/4), recording the conclusion by the equation 5/4 = 5 × (1/4).*
b. Understand a multiple of a/b as a multiple of 1/b, and use this understanding to multiply a fraction by a whole number. *For example, use a visual fraction model to express 3 × (2/5) as 6 × (1/5), recognizing this product as 6/5. (In general, n × (a/b) = (n × a)/b.)*
c. Solve word problems involving multiplication of a fraction by a whole number, e.g., by using visual fraction models and equations to represent the problem.

**4.NF.C.5.** Express a fraction with denominator 10 as an equivalent fraction with denominator 100, and use this technique to add two fractions with respective denominators 10 and 100.

**4.NF.C.6.** Use decimal notation for fractions with denominators 10 or 100.

**4.NF.C.7.** Compare two decimals to hundredths by reasoning about their size. Recognize that comparisons are valid only when the two decimals refer to the same whole. Record the results of comparisons with the symbols >, =, or <, and justify the conclusions.

## Domain 4: Measurement & Data

**4.MD.A.1.** Know relative sizes of measurement units within one system of units including km, m, cm; kg, g; lb, oz.; l, ml; hr, min, sec. Within a single system of measurement, express measurements in a larger unit in terms of a smaller unit. Record measurement equivalents in a two-column table.

**4.MD.A.2.** Use the four operations to solve word problems involving distances, intervals of time, liquid volumes, masses of objects, and money, including problems involving simple fractions or decimals, and problems that require expressing measurements given in a larger unit in terms of a smaller unit. Represent measurement quantities using diagrams such as number line diagrams that feature a measurement scale.

**4.MD.A.3.** Apply the area and perimeter formulas for rectangles in real world and mathematical problems.

**4.MD.B.4.** Make a line plot to display a data set of measurements in fractions of a unit (1/2, 1/4, 1/8). Solve problems involving addition and subtraction of fractions by using information presented in line plots.

**4.MD.C.5.** Recognize angles as geometric shapes that are formed wherever two rays share a common endpoint, and understand concepts of angle measurement:
a. An angle is measured with reference to a circle with its center at the common endpoint of the rays, by considering the fraction of the circular arc between the points where the two rays intersect the circle.
b. An angle that turns through 1/360 of a circle is called a "one-degree angle," and can be used to measure angles. An angle that turns through *n* one-degree angles is said to have an angle measure of *n* degrees.

**4.MD.C.6.** Measure angles in whole-number degrees using a protractor. Sketch angles of specified measure

**4.MD.C.7.** Recognize angle measure as additive. When an angle is decomposed into non-overlapping parts, the angle measure of the whole is the sum of the angle measures of the parts. Solve addition and subtraction problems to find unknown angles on a diagram in real world and mathematical problems.

## DOMAIN 5: GEOMETRY

**4.G.A.1.** Draw points, lines, line segments, rays, angles (right, acute, obtuse), and perpendicular and parallel lines. Identify these in two-dimensional figures.

**4.G.A.2.** Classify two-dimensional figures based on the presence or absence of parallel or perpendicular lines, or the presence or absence of angles of a specified size. Recognize right triangles as a category, and identify right triangles.

**4.G.A.3.** Recognize a line of symmetry for a two-dimensional figure as a line across the figure such that the figure can be folded along the line into matching parts. Identify line-symmetric figures and draw lines of symmetry.

## AUTHENTIC CHALLENGE PROJECTS:

STANDARD **4.NBT.A.1.** Recognize that in a multi-digit whole number, a digit in one place represents ten times what it represents in the place to its right.

**1.** Solve the following:

    **a.** 57 hundreds = _____ tens

    **b.** 830 tens = _____ hundreds

**2.** Solve the following division problems and explain the strategy you used to solve them.

    **a.** $500 \div 5 =$ _____

    **b.** $50 \div 5 =$ _____

_____

_____

_____

STANDARD **4.NBT.A.2.** Read and write multi-digit whole numbers using base-ten numerals, number names, and expanded form. Compare two multi-digit numbers based on meanings of the digits in each place, using >, =, and < symbols to record the results of comparisons.

**1.** Trent asked how many books were in the library. Mrs. Cox said that there are 97,246. Write this number in expanded form.

_____

_____

_____

**2.** Write in >, =, or < to make the following statement correct:  1,892 ◯ 1,981

1. The fourth grade classes decided to collect soda can tabs as a class project. Ms. Smith's class collected 772 tabs, Mr. Darby's class collected 887 tabs, and Ms. Bennett's class collected 802 tabs. Round the number of tabs each class collected to the nearest hundred and estimate the total number of soda can tabs collected by all three classes.

2. Mr. and Mrs. Morris saved $1,500 for their trip to the beach. They spent $428 on airline tickets. Estimate how much they have left to spend on the trip. Show your work.

1. How many tadpoles have changed into frogs if 35 tadpoles were put in the aquarium and now there are 6 tadpoles? _____

2. Tanya's team scored 1,845 points during the season and Suki's team scored 1,762 points. How many points did both teams score together? _____

1. Vanessa's dogs eat 175 pounds of food each month. How many pounds do they eat in one year? _____

2. The hospital uses 1,395 gallons of water each day. How many gallons of water will the hospital use in one week? _____

1. Solve the following division problem. Show your work. $275 \div 5$

2. Mr. Trowell went to the home improvement store and purchased a box of 1,250 nails to make flower boxes. Each box requires 8 nails. How many flower boxes can he make? Will he have any nails left over? _____ If so, how many? _____

**Standard Cluster: Generalize place value understanding for multi-digit whole numbers.**

> **STANDARD 4.NBT.A.1.** Recognize that in a multi-digit whole number, a digit in one place represents ten times what it represents in the place to its right.

**1.** Identify the number that makes this number sentence true: 4,000 = _____ hundreds

**2.** Henry has 700 baseball cards. This is ten times the number of baseball cards Steven has. How many baseball cards does Steven have? _____

**3.** After counting his money, Christopher realizes that he has ten times more money than he thought. He has $800. How much did he think he had to begin with? _____

**4.** Which statement is true?

    **a.** 40 x 100 = 400         **b.** 8,000 is ten times 80

    **c.** 720,000 is ten times 72,000     **d.** 72,000 = 10 x 720

**5.** Jeannie says she has 100 times as many songs on her computer as her brother Thomas has on his. Thomas says she only has 10 times as many. If Thomas has 200 songs and Jeannie has 2,000, who is correct? _____
Explain your answer.

_____

_____

_____

**Standard Cluster: Generalize place value understanding for multi-digit whole numbers.**

STANDARD **4.NBT.A.2.** Read and write multi-digit whole numbers using base-ten numerals, number names, and expanded form. Compare two multi-digit numbers based on meanings of the digits in each place, using >, =, and < symbols to record the results of comparisons.

**1.** Using the numeral 7,040,209

    **a.** write the expanded form.

_____

_____

    **b.** write the word form.

_____

_____

_____

    **c.** Complete the following using >, =, or <.    7,040,209 $\bigcirc$ 7,400,209

    **d.** Write the numeral: nine million, three hundred seven thousand, ninety

_____

**2.** Use the following digits to make the largest six digit number possible:

    2    5    7    9    0    2  _____

Write the number you created in word form and expanded form.

_____

_____

_____

_____

**Standard Cluster: Generalize place value understanding for multi-digit whole numbers.**

> **STANDARD 4.NBT.A.3.** Use place value understanding to round multi-digit whole numbers to any place.

1. Round 6,924,609 to the nearest:

   **a.** ten: _____

   **b.** hundred: _____

   **c.** thousand: _____

   **d.** ten thousand: _____

   **e.** hundred thousand: _____

   **f.** million: _____

2. John was absent from school the day rounding was taught. The teacher has asked you to explain to John how to round 436,299 to the nearest ten, thousand, and hundred thousand. What would you tell John?

   _____

   _____

   _____

   Round 436,299 to the nearest:

   **a.** ten: _____

   **b.** thousand: _____

   **c.** hundred thousand: _____

3. Round 57,258 to the nearest thousand. _____

**Standard Cluster: Use place value understanding
and properties of operations to perform multi-digit arithmetic.**

> STANDARD **4.NBT.B.4.** Fluently add and subtract multi-digit whole numbers using the standard algorithm.

**1.** Molly added 22,302 and 2,922 and came up with a sum of 24, 224. Mallory added the same numbers and came up with a sum of 25,224. Who is correct, Molly or Mallory? Explain your answer. _____

_____

_____

**2.** Katie's school collected pennies to donate to the local animal shelter. They collected 2,459 pennies the first week, 2,521 pennies the second week, and 3,733 pennies the third week. How many pennies did the school collect? _____

Show your work.

**3.** The school's library has 5,302 books available for student check out. If students in the school check out 1,293 books, how many books are still left in the library?

Show your work.

**4.** Katie received $180.00 for her birthday. She went to the mall and bought jeans for $34.00, a sweater for $29.90, and shoes for $52.39. How much money does Katie have left after her purchases?

_____

**5.** James has 1,079 baseball cards. Matthew has 75 more cards than James. How many cards does Matthew have?

_____

**Standard Cluster: Use place value understanding
and properties of operations to perform multi-digit arithmetic.**

> **STANDARD 4.NBT.B.5.** Multiply a whole number of up to four digits by one-digit whole number, and multiply two two-digit numbers, using strategies based on place value and the properties of operations. Illustrate and explain the calculation by using equations, rectangular arrays, and/or area models.

**1.** Margaret sold 85 bars of candy for her organization. If each bar of candy costs $2.00, how much money did Margaret collect? Explain the strategy you used to solve the problem. _____

_____

_____

**2.** Mrs. Waltrip wrote the following four numbers on the board: 2, 7, 5 and 3. She challenged her class to use these numbers to write a two-digit by two-digit multiplication problem that would result in the largest possible product. Write and solve the multiplication problem that would result in the largest possible product using 2, 7, 5, and 3.

_____

_____

**3.** Lucy looked over the donut display in the local bakery. There were 12 rows of donuts with 24 donuts in each row. How many donuts were in the case? Show your work.

**4.** Nina's dad drives a truck for a moving company. Each day, Monday through Friday, he drives 327 miles. How many miles does he drive each week? _____

**5.** The 4th, 5th, and 6th grade classes are going to watch a play at the local college. The auditorium has 48 rows with 60 seats in each row. How many seats are in the auditorium? _____

**Standard Cluster: Use place value understanding
and properties of operations to perform multi-digit arithmetic.**

> **STANDARD 4.NBT.B.6.** Find whole-number quotients and remainders with up to four-digit dividends and one-digit divisors, using strategies based on place value, the properties of operations, and/or the relationship between multiplication and division. Illustrate and explain the calculation by using equations, rectangular arrays, and/or area models.

**1.** Stan and his two brothers collected 351 soda cans to be recycled. If each boy takes an equal number of cans to the recycling plant, how many soda cans will each boy take?

_____

**2.** Tammy and four of her friends won four dozen cookies at the auction. If they split the cookies evenly, how many cookies will each girl get? Will there be any left over? Explain your answer. _____

_____

_____

**3.** There are 125 students in the fourth grade at Somewhere Elementary. If there are 5 classrooms, how many students are in each class? Check your answer using multiplication. Show your work.

**4. a.** Hannah bought a roll of ribbon to make hair bows. If the roll contained 120 inches of ribbon and each hair bow requires 9 inches, how many hair bows can she make? _____

**b.** If Hannah buys enough rolls to have 1,625 inches of ribbon, how much will she have left over if she makes as many ribbons as possible? _____

# Grade 4 Domain 3 | Number & Operations—Fractions

**STANDARD 4.NF.A.1.** Explain why a fraction a/b is equivalent to a fraction (n × a)/(n × b) by using visual fraction models, with attention to how the number and size of the parts differ even though the two fractions themselves are the same size. Use this principle to recognize and generate equivalent fractions.

**1.** Find 3 additional equivalent fractions:

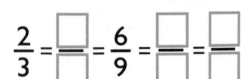

$$\frac{2}{3} = \frac{\phantom{0}}{\phantom{0}} = \frac{6}{9} = \frac{\phantom{0}}{\phantom{0}} = \frac{\phantom{0}}{\phantom{0}}$$

**2.** Which fraction is equivalent to $\frac{3}{4}$ ?

a. $\frac{9}{10}$    b. $\frac{5}{8}$    c. $\frac{6}{8}$    d. $\frac{12}{15}$

**STANDARD 4.NF.A.2.** Compare two fractions with different numerators and different denominators, e.g., by creating common denominators or numerators, or by comparing to a benchmark fraction such as 1/2. Recognize that comparisons are valid only when the two fractions refer to the same whole. Record the results of comparisons with symbols >, =, or <, and justify the conclusions, e.g., by using a visual fraction model.

**1.** Fill in the circle with >, =, or <.

a. $\frac{3}{8}$ ◯ $\frac{1}{2}$    b. $\frac{4}{5}$ ◯ $\frac{1}{2}$    c. $\frac{5}{10}$ ◯ $\frac{1}{2}$    d. $\frac{2}{3}$ ◯ $\frac{1}{2}$

**2.** Which fraction is greater than $\frac{4}{5}$?    a. $\frac{2}{6}$    b. $\frac{8}{10}$    c. $\frac{2}{3}$    d. $\frac{13}{15}$

**STANDARD 4.NF.B.3.** Understand a fraction a/b with a > 1 as a sum of fractions 1/b.
a. Understand addition and subtraction of fr actions as joining and separating parts referring to the same whole.
b. Decompose a fraction into a sum of fractions with the same denominator in more than one way, recording each decomposition by an equation.
c. Add and subtract mixed numbers with like denominators, e.g., by replacing each mixed number with an equivalent fraction, and/or by using properties of operations and the relationship between addition and subtraction.
d. Solve word problems involving addition and subtraction of fractions referring to the same whole and having like denominators, e.g., by using visual fraction models and equations to represent the problem.

**1.** Add the following mixed numbers. Show your work.

$$1\frac{1}{5} + 2\frac{2}{5} = \underline{\phantom{0000}}$$

**2.** Ted added $\frac{1}{4} + \frac{2}{4}$ and got $\frac{3}{8}$. Amy says the answer is $\frac{3}{4}$. Who is correct? _____
Explain using a model.

STANDARD **4.NF.B.4.** Apply and extend previous understandings of multiplication to multiply a fraction by a whole number.
a. Understand a fraction a/b as a multiple of 1/b. For example, use a visual fraction model to represent 5/4 as the product 5 × (1/4), recording the conclusion by the equation 5/4 = 5 × (1/4).
b. Understand a multiple of a/b as a multiple of 1/b, and use this understanding to multiply a fraction by a whole number.
c. Solve word problems involving multiplication of a fraction by a whole number, e.g., by using visual fraction models and equations to represent the problem.

**1.** Annie has 3 candy bars each divided into four pieces. She wants to give three pieces to Mark, Callie, James, and Marianne. Will she have enough pieces? _____ Explain.

_____

_____

**2.** Mrs. Appleton wants to give each of the students in her class $\frac{1}{2}$ of a banana to make banana splits. If she has 22 students, how many bananas will she need? _____

STANDARD **4.NF.C.5.** Express a fraction with denominator 10 as an equivalent fraction with denominator 100, and use this technique to add two fractions with respective denominators 10 and 100.

**1.** Add: $\dfrac{40}{100} + \dfrac{5}{10} =$ _____

**2.** Find the sum: $\dfrac{3}{10} + \dfrac{60}{100} =$ _____

**1.** Label the number line with equivalent fractions and decimals.

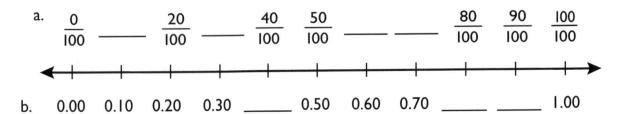

a.  $\dfrac{0}{100}$  —— $\dfrac{20}{100}$ —— $\dfrac{40}{100}$  $\dfrac{50}{100}$  —— —— $\dfrac{80}{100}$  $\dfrac{90}{100}$  $\dfrac{100}{100}$

b.   0.00   0.10   0.20   0.30 _____ 0.50   0.60   0.70 _____ _____ 1.00

**2.** Which number sentence is correct?

**a.** $.57 = \dfrac{57}{1000}$    **b.** $\dfrac{3}{4}$ and .75    **c.** $\dfrac{5}{8}$ and .25    **d.** $.7$ and $\dfrac{7}{100}$

**1.** Compare using <, >, or =.

**a.** $0.23$ ◯ $\dfrac{32}{100}$    **b.** $\dfrac{57}{100}$ ◯ $0.57$    **c.** $0.7$ ◯ $\dfrac{70}{100}$

**2.** Name five decimals that will make this number sentence true: _____ < .45
Explain how you know the number sentence is true.

_____  _____  _____  _____  _____

_____

_____

_____

**Standard Cluster: Extend understanding of fraction equivalence and ordering.**

STANDARD **4.NF.A.1.** Explain why a fraction a/b is equivalent to a fraction (n x a)/(n x b) by using visual fraction models, with attention to how the number and size of the parts differ even though the two fractions themselves are the same size. Use this principle to recognize and generate equivalent fractions.

**1.** Complete the following pattern of equivalent fractions – fill in the missing denominator:

$$\frac{1}{2} = \frac{2}{4} = \frac{3}{6} = \frac{4}{\square}$$

**2.** Jay, Jason, and Jon won a cake at the cakewalk. They decide to divide the cake into equal parts so that each boy receives an equal share. Show three ways they can divide the cake into equal parts. Write the fraction below each cake.

$\bigcirc$   $\bigcirc$   $\bigcirc$

_____   _____   _____

**3.** Stella and Angelica bought packs of bubblegum with their allowance. After chewing a few pieces, the girls decided to save the rest of their bubblegum for later. Stella saved $\frac{3}{4}$ of her bubblegum. Angelica saved $\frac{6}{8}$ of her bubblegum. Which girl saved more bubblegum? _____

Explain your answer. _____

_____

_____

_____

**4.** Find the equivalent fractional parts that are shaded.

**a.**

_____

**b.**

_____

**c.**

_____

**5.** Divide each circle into equivalent parts and shade to equal $\frac{1}{4}$.

**Standard Cluster: Extend understanding of fraction equivalence and ordering.**

> **STANDARD 4.NF.A.2.** Compare two fractions with different numerators and different denominators, e.g., by creating common denominators or numerators, or by comparing to a benchmark fraction such as 1/2. Recognize that comparisons are valid only when the two fractions refer to the same whole. Record the results of comparisons with symbols, >, =, or <, and justify the conclusions, e.g., by using a visual fraction model.

**1.** Circle the pictures that show equivalent fractions for $\frac{1}{2}$.

**2.** Place the following fractions in the correct order from least to greatest:

$\frac{2}{3}$  $\frac{1}{2}$  $\frac{5}{6}$  _____

**3.** Donna and Kay were working on a math problem. Donna said that $\frac{7}{8}$ is smaller than $\frac{7}{12}$ because 12 is larger than 8. Do you agree with Donna? _____ Explain your answer.

_____

_____

**4.** Josie and Erica each ordered a medium pizza. Josie ate $\frac{3}{4}$ of her pizza and Erica ate $\frac{5}{8}$ of hers. Who ate the most pizza? _____ Explain your answer.

_____

_____

**5.** Create fractions with common denominators for $\frac{3}{4}$ and $\frac{4}{5}$. _____

**Standard Cluster: Build fractions from unit fractions by applying and extending previous understandings of operations on whole numbers.**

---

**STANDARD 4.NF.B.3** Understand a fraction a/b with a > 1 as a sum of fractions 1/b.
  a. Understand addition and subtraction of fractions as joining and separating parts referring to the same whole.
  b. Decompose a fraction into a sum of fractions with the same denominator in more than one way, recording each decomposition by an equation. Justify decompositions, e.g., by using a visual fraction model.
  *Examples: 3/8 = 1/8 + 1/8 + 1/8 ; 3/8 = 1/8 + 2/8 ; 2 1/8 = 1 + 1 + 1/8 = 8/8 + 8/8 + 1/8.*
  c. Add and subtract mixed numbers with like denominators, e.g., by replacing each mixed number with an equivalent fraction, and/or by using properties of operations and the relationship between addition and subtraction.
  d. Solve word problems involving addition and subtraction of fractions referring to the same whole and having like denominators, e.g., by using visual fraction models and equations to represent the problem.

---

**1.** Charles bought a pizza for dinner. He ate $\frac{3}{8}$ of the pizza for dinner and another $\frac{2}{8}$ of the pizza before going to bed. How much pizza does Charles have left?
Show your work. _____

**2.** Show two different ways you can add fractions to reach the sum of $2\frac{1}{2}$.

_____

_____

**3.** Nina is making cookies for her mom's birthday and wanted to see how much flour she would need. The chocolate chip cookies require $2\frac{1}{4}$ cups of flour and the peanut butter cookies require $1\frac{2}{4}$ cups of flour.
How much flour will Nina need to make both kinds of cookies? _____

**4.** Molly feeds her cat $\frac{1}{3}$ cup of food in the morning and $\frac{1}{3}$ cup in the evening. How much food does she feed her cat each day?

**5.** Susan baked two pans of brownies, one round pan and one square pan. Each pan was cut into 4 pieces. If Susan ate one piece from each pan, did she eat $\frac{2}{4}$ of the brownies? Explain using the model below.

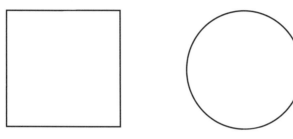

_____

_____

_____

**6.** Write $\frac{7}{8}$ as a sum of fractions three different ways.

_____     _____     _____

**Standard Cluster: Build fractions from unit fractions by applying and extending previous understandings of operations on whole numbers.**

**STANDARD 4.NF.B.4** Apply and extend previous understandings of multiplication to multiply a fraction by a whole number.

a. Understand a fraction a/b as a multiple of 1/b. *For example, use a visual fraction model to represent 5/4 as the product 5 × (1/4), recording the conclusion by the equation 5/4 = 5 × (1/4).*

b. Understand a multiple of a/b as a multiple of 1/b, and use this understanding to multiply a fraction by a whole number. *For example, use a visual fraction model to express 3 × (2/5) as 6 × (1/5), recognizing this product as 6/5. (In general, n × (a/b) = (n × a)/b.)*

c. Solve word problems involving multiplication of a fraction by a whole number, e.g., by using visual fraction models and equations to represent the problem. *For example, if each person at a party will eat 3/8 of a pound of roast beef, and there will be 5 people at the party, how many pounds of roast beef will be needed? Between what two whole numbers does your answer lie?*

**1.** Multiply the following: $4 \times \frac{1}{3}$. Write your answer as a mixed number or improper fraction. Draw a model to show how your answer should look.

**2.** Tommy is allowed to watch $3\frac{1}{2}$ hours of television each week. If he watches $\frac{1}{2}$ hour of television each day, will he be able to watch television each day of the week? _____

**3.** Hannah's soccer coach requires each player to practice $\frac{3}{4}$ hour each day. How much time does Hannah practice soccer each week? _____

**4.** Use the model to complete the equations and represent $\frac{4}{5}$ as $4 \times \frac{1}{5}$.

| $\frac{1}{5}$ | $\frac{1}{5}$ | $\frac{1}{5}$ | $\frac{1}{5}$ | $\frac{1}{5}$ |
|---|---|---|---|---|

$\frac{4}{5} = $ ____ $+$ ____ $+$ ____ $+$ ____      $\frac{4}{5} = $ ____ $\times \frac{1}{5}$

**5.** Harry's baseball team is having a picnic and his mom is baking chocolate chip cookies. Each batch requires $\frac{3}{4}$ cup of chocolate chips and Harry's mom needs to make 5 batches.

How many cups of chocolate chips will she need?_____

If each bag holds 2 cups, how many bags will she need? _____

**Standard Cluster: Understand decimal notation for fractions, and compare decimal fractions.**

STANDARD **4.NF.C.5** Express a fraction with denominator 10 as an equivalent fraction with denominator 100, and use this technique to add two fractions with respective denominators 10 and 100. For example, express 3/10 as 30/100, and add 3/10 + 4/100 = 34/100.

**1.** Add the following fractions: $\frac{3}{10} + \frac{60}{100}$ _____

**2.** Matthew's goal is to collect 100 trading cards. He has already collected $\frac{2}{10}$ of his goal. How many hundredths does he have? _____

**3.** Katie and Rebekah weeded their family's vegetable garden. Katie weeded $\frac{3}{10}$ of the garden and Rebekah weeded $\frac{40}{100}$ of the garden. How much of the garden did Katie and Rebekah weed? _____

**4.** Daniel spent the day painting his room. He used $\frac{7}{10}$ gallon of paint. How many hundredths of a gallon did he use?
Complete the model to find your answer.

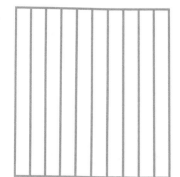 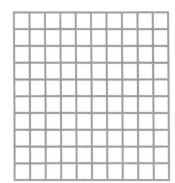 _____

**5.** Joanie and Karen's mom gave them $10 each to spend at the mall. Joanie spent $\frac{6}{10}$ of her $10 and Karen spent $\frac{90}{100}$ of hers. How much money did they spend all together? _____

**Standard Cluster: Understand decimal notation for fractions, and compare decimal fractions.**

> **STANDARD 4.NF.C.6** Use decimal notation for fractions with denominators 10 or 100. For example, rewrite 0.62 as 62/100; describe a length as 0.62 meters; locate 0.62 on a number line diagram.

**1.** Christina ran $\frac{75}{100}$ mile at the track meet. Write $\frac{75}{100}$ as a decimal. _____

**2.** Complete the following number line with the correct decimals and fractions.

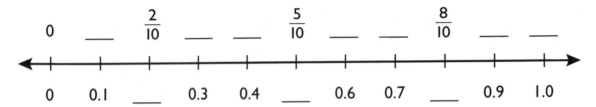

**3.** Wally grew 0.55 inch last year. Write how much he grew as a fraction. _____

**4.** Monday morning, the weatherman said it rained 0.95 of an inch the night before.

Write 0.95 as a fraction. _____

**5.** Allison wrote a report on zebras for her science class. She filled $\frac{73}{100}$ of her flash drive with information. Write how much she filled the flash drive as a decimal. _____

**Standard Cluster: Understand decimal notation for fractions, and compare decimal fractions.**

STANDARD **4.NF.C.7.** Compare two decimals to hundredths by reasoning about their size. Recognize that comparisons are valid only when the two decimals refer to the same whole. Record the results of comparisons with the symbols >, =, or <, and justify the conclusions, e.g., by using a visual model.

**1.** Place the following numbers in order from least to greatest:

0.33      0.03      0.40      0.30

_____    _____    _____    _____

**2.** Compare the following decimals using >, =, or <

0.24 ◯ 0.42        0.40 ◯ 0.4        1.33 ◯ 0.75

**3.** Satcha hiked 5.25 miles and Milo hiked 4.95 miles. Who hiked farther, Satcha or Milo? Explain how you solved the problem.

_____

_____

_____

**4.** Joe, Bill, and Eddie had a running contest. Joe ran 0.67 mile, Bill ran 0.59 mile, and Eddie ran 0.9 mile without stopping. Which statement is true?

**a.** 0.67 > 0.9      **b.** 0.59 > 0.67      **c.** 0.9 > 0.67      **d.** 0.59 > 0.9

**5.** Fill in the circle with >, =, or <. Use the models to find your answer.

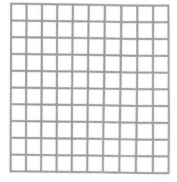 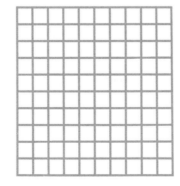

0.75 ◯ 0.82

# Grade 4 Domain 4 | Measurement & Data

**STANDARD 4.MD.A.1.** Know relative sizes of measurement units within one system of units including km, m, cm; kg, g; lb, oz.; l, ml; hr, min, sec. Within a single system of measurement, express measurements in a larger unit in terms of a smaller unit. Record measurement equivalents in a two-column table.

**1.** Darby is helping her dad make pancakes. The recipe calls for 4 tablespoons of sugar. How many teaspoons will this be? _____

**2.** Janet's favorite show is coming on in $2\frac{1}{2}$ hours. How many minutes is this? _____

**STANDARD 4.MD.A.2.** Use the four operations to solve word problems involving distances, intervals of time, liquid volumes, masses of objects, and money, including problems involving simple fractions or decimals, and problems that require expressing measurements given in a larger unit in terms of a smaller unit. Represent measurement quantities using diagrams such as number line diagrams that feature a measurement scale.

**1.** Austin's baby brother is one year, 5 weeks and 3 days old. Ellie's baby brother is 399 days old. Whose baby brother is older, Austin or Ellie's? How much older is he? _____

**2.** Nancy Ann lives 2.2 miles away from the school. Matthew lives $2\frac{1}{4}$ miles away from school. Who lives closer to school, Nancy Ann or Matthew? _____

**STANDARD 4.MD.A.3.** Apply the area and perimeter formulas for rectangles in real world and mathematical problems.

**1.** Mrs. Knight is replacing the carpet in her office. Her office is 10 feet wide and 8 feet long. The carpet she chose is $7.00 per square foot. How much will Mrs. Knight's new carpet cost? _____

**2.** Caroline has a pencil box that has a perimeter of 30 centimeters and an area of 50 square centimeters. What are the dimensions of Caroline's pencil box?

_____

STANDARD **4.MD.B.4.** Make a line plot to display a data set of measurements in fractions of a unit (1/2, 1/4, 1/8). Solve problems involving addition and subtraction of fractions by using information presented in line plots.

**1.** The students in Mrs. Tyson's class recorded their favorite pets on the line plot below. Use the line plot to solve:

### FAVORITE PETS

```
                  X
    X             X
    X             X                   X
    X             X                   X
    X             X          X        X         X
    X             X          X        X         X         X
  ─────────────────────────────────────────────────────────────
    cat          dog        bird    hamster    fish      hermit
                                                          crabs
```

What fraction of the students like birds and hamsters?  _____

**2.** Tony and Tamara surveyed their classmates to determine the amount of time spent doing homework the night before. The results are recorded in the table beside:

| Sifa | 1 hour |
|---|---|
| Priya | $\frac{1}{2}$ hour |
| Marci | $\frac{3}{4}$ hour |
| Frank | $\frac{1}{4}$ hour |
| Starla | $\frac{1}{3}$ hour |
| Harry | $\frac{1}{2}$ hour |
| Steve | $\frac{1}{3}$ hour |
| Joe | $\frac{5}{12}$ hour |
| Maggie | $\frac{1}{6}$ hour |

Use the data in the table to complete the following line plot below:

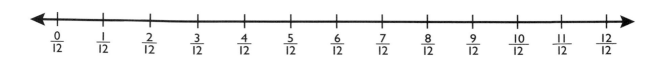

$$\frac{0}{12} \quad \frac{1}{12} \quad \frac{2}{12} \quad \frac{3}{12} \quad \frac{4}{12} \quad \frac{5}{12} \quad \frac{6}{12} \quad \frac{7}{12} \quad \frac{8}{12} \quad \frac{9}{12} \quad \frac{10}{12} \quad \frac{11}{12} \quad \frac{12}{12}$$

> **STANDARD 4.MD.C.5.** Recognize angles as geometric shapes that are formed wherever two rays share a common endpoint, and understand concepts of angle measurement: An angle is measured with reference to a circle with its center at the common endpoint of the rays, by considering the fraction of the circular arc between the points where the two rays intersect the circle. An angle that turns through 1/360 of a circle is called a "one-degree angle," and can be used to measure angles. An angle that turns through n one-degree angles is said to have an angle measure of n degrees.

**1.** How many degrees are in an angle that turns through half of a circle? _____

**2.** Fred cut a pie into six pieces. Use the fractional part to determine the angle of each piece. _____

> **STANDARD 4.MD.C.6.** Measure angles in whole-number degrees using a protractor. Sketch angles of specified measure.

**1.** Use a protractor to determine the degree of the following angle.

_____

**2.** Use a protractor to draw an angle with a measure of 70 degrees.

STANDARD **4.MD.C.7.** Recognize angle measure as additive. When an angle is decomposed into non-overlapping parts, the angle measure of the whole is the sum of the angle measures of the parts. Solve addition and subtraction problems to find unknown angles on a diagram in real world and mathematical problems.

**1.** If a right angle is broken into two equal non-overlapping angles, what is the measure of each angle? _____

**2.** Madison, Sally, and Maggie ordered a pizza during their sleepover. The measure of the angle for each slice of pizza was 35 degrees. If each girl ate 2 slices of pizza, what is the measure of the angle made by the amount of pizza eaten by each girl? _____

**Standard Cluster: Solve problems involving measurement and conversion of measurements from a larger unit to a smaller unit.**

STANDARD **4.MD.A.1.** Know relative sizes of measurement units within one system of units including km, m, cm; kg, g; lb. oz.; l, ml; hr, min, sec. Within a single system of measurement, express measurements in a larger unit in terms of a smaller unit. Record measurement equivalents in a two-column table.

**1.** Robert is recording the length of his shadow at different times of the day. At 3:00 p.m., his shadow measured 2 meters. How many centimeters is this? _____
Explain how you know this.

_____

_____

_____

**2.** Complete the table.

| 5 feet | _____ inches |
|---|---|
| 18 feet | _____ yards |
| 2 yards | _____ inches |
| 20 feet | _____ inches |
| 36 inches | _____ yards |

**3.** The school day at Smithville Elementary School is 7 hours. How many minutes is this?

a. 420          b. 2,100          c. 4,200          d. 210

**4.** Marge bought 10 pounds of sugar to make fudge for Christmas. How many ounces of sugar did she buy? _____ Explain.

_____

_____

**5.** Hannah is 55 inches tall. Hannah's mom is 5 feet 4 inches tall. Who is taller, Hannah or her mom? _____ How do you know?

_____

_____

_____

**Standard Cluster: Solve problems involving measurement and conversion of measurements from a larger unit to a smaller unit.**

STANDARD **4.MD.A.2.** Use four operations to solve word problems involving distances, intervals of time, liquid volumes, masses of objects, and money, including problems involving simple fractions or decimals, and problems that require expressing measurements given in a larger unit in terms of a smaller unit. Represent measurement quantities using diagrams such as number line diagrams that feature a measurement scale.

**1.** Dorian lives $4\frac{3}{4}$ miles from school. Ann Marie lives 4.7 miles from school. Who lives closer to school? _____

How much closer? _____

**2.** Marcy has 3 quarts of milk in the refrigerator. Her mom brings home another gallon. How many quarts of milk do they have now? _____

**3.** Janice is babysitting on the weekends. If she makes $55 each weekend, how much will she make in 7 weekends? _____

**4.** Anthony took his dog Bella to the vet for a checkup. Bella weighed 12.2 pounds. Last checkup Bella weighed 10.9 pounds. How much weight has she gained? _____

**5.** Lauren is making punch for her birthday party. Her punch bowl holds 4 gallons of liquid. How many **quarts** of liquid does the punch bowl hold? How many **cups** would that be? _____

**Standard Cluster: Solve problems involving measurement and conversion
of measurements from a larger unit to a smaller unit.**

> **STANDARD 4.MD.A.3.** Apply the area and perimeter formulas for rectangles in real world and mathematical problems.

**1.** Find the area and perimeter of this object.

7m

13m

_____

**2.** Janae is redecorating her room. She wants to put a
wallpaper border on the walls. Her room measures 10
feet x 15 feet. If the wallpaper border comes in rolls of 10
feet, how many rolls will she need to complete her room? _____

**3.** The school's PTO is planning fundraisers to buy a fence to go around the playground. If
the playground has the following measurements, how much fencing will be needed?

46 yds

75 yds

_____

**4.** New carpet is being ordered for the music room. If the perimeter
of the rectangular room is 110 ft and one wall measures 25 ft, how
many square feet of carpet should be ordered?

_____

**5.** Find the area and perimeter of the following object:

7 feet

7 feet

_____

STANDARD **4.MD.B.4.** Make a line plot to display a data set of measurements in fractions of a unit. Solve problems involving addition and subtraction of fractions by using information presented in line plots.

**1.** Mrs. Jackson's class made the line plot to show how many books the students read last month. What fraction of the students read 4 or more books?

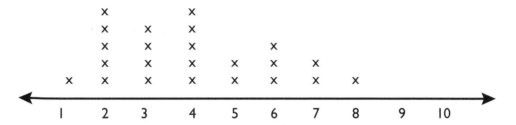

**2.** Using the line plot from number 1, which statement below is true? _____

    **a.** The fraction of students who read more than 4 books is more than those who read less than 4 books.

    **b.** The fraction of students reading the most and least number of books is the same.

    **c.** The fraction of students who read six books is more than the fraction of students who read three books.

    **d.** The sum of the fractions of those reading 5 and 6 books is more than the fraction of those who read 2 books.

**3.** Angelina surveyed her class to find out their favorite candy. The results were:

| Candy | Fraction of Students Who Like as Favorite |
|---|---|
| Reese's | $\frac{9}{19}$ |
| Air Heads | $\frac{3}{19}$ |
| Sourpatch Kids | $\frac{5}{19}$ |
| M & M's | $\frac{2}{19}$ |

Make a line plot to display Angelina's results.

       Reese's     Air Heads     Sourpatch Kids     M & Ms

4. Maggie works at a horse farm and feeds the horses each day. She recorded the amount of feed eaten by the horses on the line plot below:

Bushels of Feed

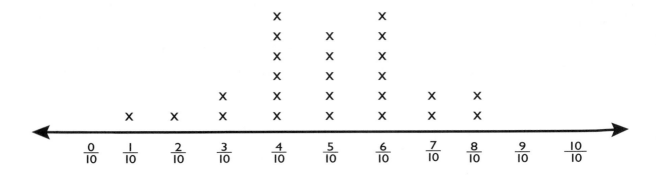

a. What is the total amount of bushels of feed that was eaten by horses that ate $\frac{5}{10}$ bushel? _____

b. How much more is the total amount of feed that was eaten by horses that ate $\frac{6}{10}$ bushels than those who ate $\frac{4}{10}$ bushel? _____

5. Coach Boone recorded the amount of time her players spent practicing foot skills after yesterday's soccer practice. She listed the results in the table below.

| Student | Amount of Time |
|---------|----------------|
| Francis | $\frac{1}{4}$ hour |
| Jada | $\frac{1}{2}$ hour |
| Kari | 0 hour |
| Terri | 1 hour |
| Fran | $\frac{1}{2}$ hour |
| Paulette | $\frac{1}{4}$ hour |
| Sophie | $\frac{1}{2}$ hour |
| Allison | $\frac{3}{4}$ hour |

Create a line plot of Coach Boone's results.

**Standard Cluster: Geometric measurement:**
**understand concepts of angle and measure angles.**

STANDARD **4.MD.C.5.** Recognize angles as geometric shapes that are formed wherever two rays share a common endpoint, and understand concepts of angle measurement:

a. An angle is measured with reference to a circle with its center at the common endpoint of the rays, by considering the fraction of the circular arc between the points where the two rays intersect the circle. An angle that turns through 1/360 of a circle is called a "one-degree angle," and can be used to measure angles.

b. An angle that turns through n one-degree angles is said to have an angle measure of n degrees.

**1.** A 75 degree angle turns through what fraction of a circle? _____

**2.** Draw a time on the clock where the hour and minute hand form a 90⁰ angle.

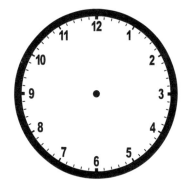

**3.** What is the measure of this angle?

    **a.** 90⁰    **b.** it cannot be measured    **c.** 180⁰    **d.** it is not an angle

**4.** Identify each of the following as a line, line segment, or ray.

    **a.**  _____

    **b.** _____

    **c.** _____

**5.** Angle X measures 145 degrees. If Angle Y measures 90 degrees, what is the measure of Angle Z?

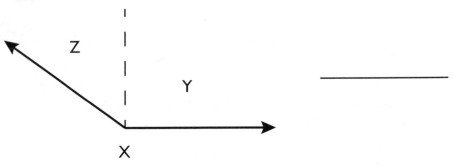

---

STANDARD **4.MD.C.6.** Measure angles in whole-number degrees using a protractor. Sketch angles of specified measure.

---

**1.** Use a protractor to measure the angle.

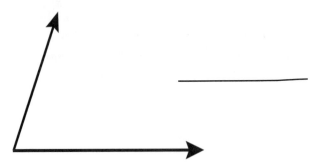

**2.** Which angle measures 40⁰?  _____

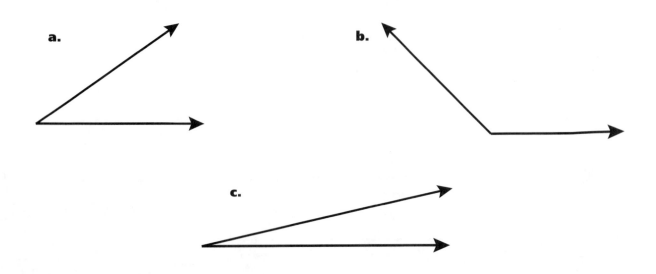

**3.** Use a protractor to draw a 105⁰ angle.

**4.** Measure the angle formed by the hour and minute hands on the clock.

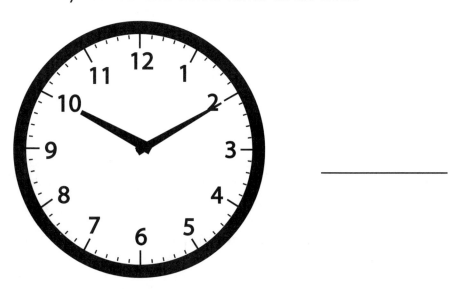

_____

**5.** Jimmy measured the angle as 70 degrees that was actually 110 degrees. Explain Jimmy's error.

_____

_____

_____

_____

**Standard Cluster: Geometric measurement:**
**understand concepts of angle and measure angles.**

STANDARD **4.MD.C.7.** Recognize angle measure as additive. When an angle is decomposed into non-overlapping parts, the angle measure of the whole is the sum of the angle measures of the parts. Solve addition and subtraction problems to find unknown angles on a diagram in real world and mathematical problems, e.g., by using an equation with a symbol for the unknown angle measure.

**1.** What is the measure of the unknown angle? _____

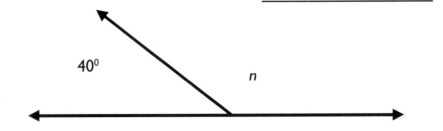

$40^0$

$n$

**2.** Donald divided a $90^0$ angle into two angles.
   Name two angles into which he could have divided the angle.

   _____        _____

**3.** James has one cookie. He is dividing it into three equal pieces to share
   with his two friends. What is the angle of each piece of the cookie?  _____

**4.** The time showing on a clock is 7:00. After 15 minutes, how
   many degrees has the minute hand moved?
   _____

**5.** The teacher asked Tommy to draw an angle that measured 80 degrees then
   break the 80 degree angle into two non-overlapping angles. If one of Tommy's
   angles measures 55 degrees, what is the measure of his other angle?  _____

# Grade 4 Domain 5 | Geometry

**STANDARD 4.G.A.1.** Draw points, lines, line segments, rays, angles (right, acute, obtuse), and perpendicular and parallel lines. Identify these in two-dimensional figures.

**1.** Draw a figure that has both perpendicular and parallel lines. Label each.

**2.** Is the following a line, line segment, or ray?

_____

**STANDARD 4.G.A.2.** Classify two-dimensional figures based on the presence or absence of parallel or perpendicular lines, or the presence or absence of angles of a specified size. Recognize right triangles as a category, and identify right triangles.

**1.** Classify the triangle as right, obtuse, or acute.  _____

**2.** How many obtuse angles are in this triangle?  _____

**STANDARD 4.G.A.3.** Recognize a line of symmetry for a two-dimensional figure as a line across the figure such that the figure can be folded along the line into matching parts. Identify line-symmetric figures and draw lines of symmetry.

**1.** Circle the figures that have lines of symmetry.

**2.** Draw a shape that has no lines of symmetry.

**Standard Cluster: Draw and identify lines and angles,
and classify shapes by properties of their lines and angles.**

**STANDARD 4.G.A.1.** Draw points, lines, line segments, rays, angles (right, acute, obtuse), and perpendicular and parallel lines. Identify these in two-dimensional figures.

**1.** Identify the following figure.

     **a.** point      **b.** ray      **c.** line      **d.** line segment

**2.** Draw the angle.  **a.** right angle     **b.** obtuse angle     **c.** acute angle

**3.** Identify the type of lines as perpendicular, intersecting, or parallel.

  **a.** 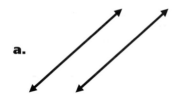     **b.**      **c.**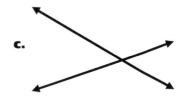

_____  _____  _____

**4.** Classify the following angles as acute, obtuse, right or straight line.

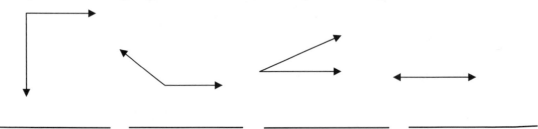

_____  _____  _____  _____

**5.** Use a red crayon to trace two parallel lines in the figure below.

# Grade 4 Domain 5 | Geometry

**Standard Cluster: Draw and identify lines and angles, and classify shapes by properties of their lines and angles.**

**STANDARD 4.G.A.2.** Classify two-dimensional figures based on the presence or absence of parallel or perpendicular lines, or the presence or absence of angles of a specified size. Recognize right triangles as a category, and identify right triangles.

**1.** Is this a parallelogram? ________ Explain how you know.

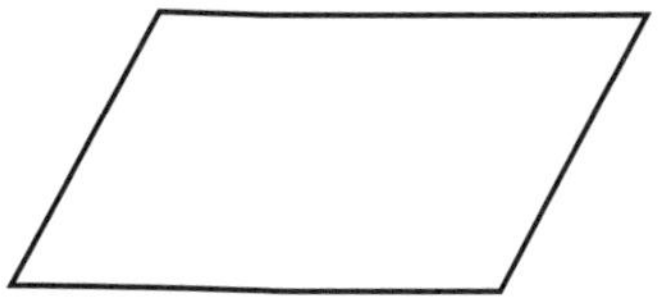

______________________________________________

______________________________________________

______________________________________________

**2.** What kind of lines form a rectangle? ______________________________

**3.** Josiah drew the following shape:

Describe the angles in this shape.

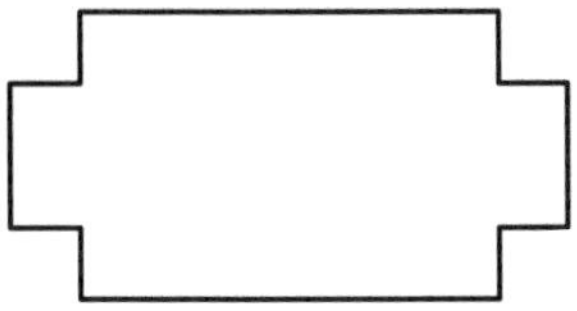

______________________________________________

______________________________________________

______________________________________________

**4.** Is a rectangle a square? ________ Explain your rationale.

______________________________________________

______________________________________________

______________________________________________

**5.** Which of the following figures does not have any perpendicular lines?

**a.** 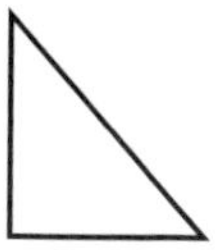

**b.** 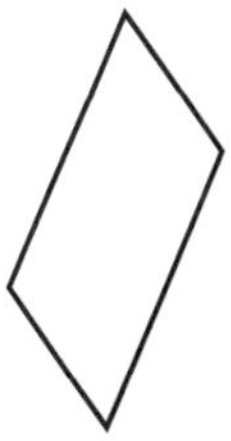

**c.** 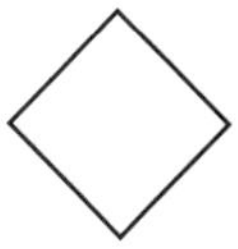

**d.** 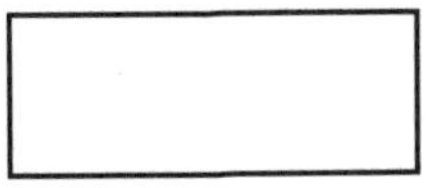

> **STANDARD 4.G.A.3.** Recognize a line of symmetry for a two-dimensional figure as a line across the figure such that the figure can be folded along the line into matching parts. Identify line-symmetric figures and draw lines of symmetry.

**1.** Circle the letters that have a line of symmetry.

A B C D E F G H I J K L M N O P Q R S T U V W X Y Z

**2.** Draw all lines of symmetry.

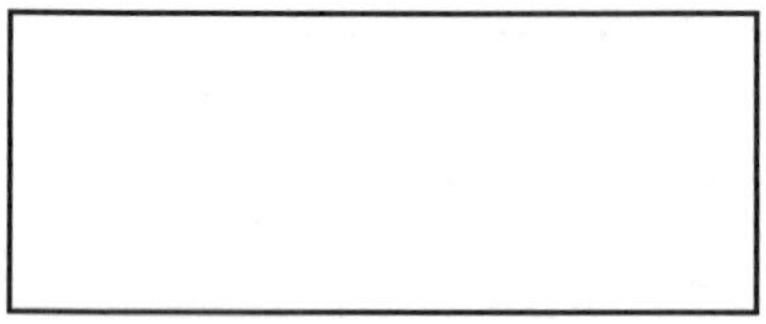

**3.** Match the figure to the number of lines of symmetry.

**a.** 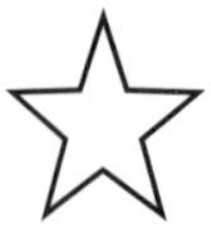 ☆          1 line

**b.** 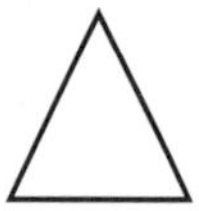 △          2 lines

**c.** 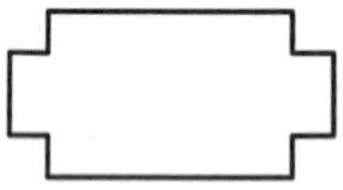 ⬚          5 lines

**4.** How many lines of symmetry does a circle have? _____ Explain.

_____

**5.** Does the following figure have a line of symmetry?
How do you know?

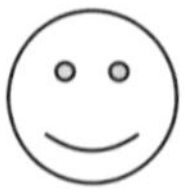

_____

_____

**6.** Christine said this equilateral triangle has 2 lines of symmetry.

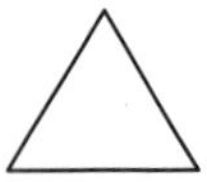

Do you agree with Christine? _____

How many lines of symmetry does this polygon have? _____

# Authentic Challenge Projects:
# Technology Infused Math Extensions

This section profiles three math projects or classroom tasks. Each project is designed to include four major principles: higher-level thinking, technology integration, authentic connections, and engaged learning.

HIGHER-LEVEL THINKING: With each of these tasks students are thinking at the highest cognitive levels by applying, analyzing, evaluating, and creating.

TECHNOLOGY INTEGRATION: Each of the tasks also includes technology integration. Technology is a part of society and career workforce skills. Often students spend a large amount of their time using technology outside school, yet inside schools technology is not being used during the learning process. These projects or classroom tasks naturally embed technology into the teaching-learning process.

AUTHENTIC CONNECTIONS: To clearly connect to the real world, each project or instructional task has connections with other subject areas and/or real-world topics.

ENGAGED LEARNING: In each of the projects the goal is for students to be focused and engaged in the learning. Students are encouraged to collaborate with others to create these projects and classroom tasks

Each of the math projects has three sections: Assignment Overview, Task Description, and Sample Student Work.

ASSIGNMENT OVERVIEW: At the beginning of each of the three projects, the standards are identified along with learning objectives and technology needed for the project.

TASK DESCRIPTION: The Task Description sheets are meant to be copied and distributed to students along with the rubric or mastery checklist to guide their creation of the project.

SAMPLE STUDENT WORK: A sample of student work is provided to show how a typical student might complete the project. The teacher may decide to share this with the students or not.

# PLAN A FAMILY TRIP

## Standards

### NUMBER & OPERATIONS – FRACTIONS

**4.OA.A.3:** Solve multistep word problems posed with whole numbers and having whole-number answers using the four operations, including problems in which remainders must be interpreted. Represent these problems using equations with a letter standing for the unknown quantity. Assess the reasonableness of answers using mental computation and estimation strategies including rounding.

### OPERATIONS & ALGEBRAIC THINKING

**4.NF.C.7:** Compare two decimals to hundredths by reasoning about their size. Recognize that comparisons are valid only when the two decimals refer to the same whole. Record the results of comparisons with the symbols >, =, or <, and justify the conclusions.

## Learning Objectives

• Students will create a budget for two educational family trips using their skills of addition, multiplication, and division.

• Students will design a video persuading their family to go on this trip.

## Plan a Family Trip Project Tasks

**1.** Select two destinations that are no more than five hours away from your house. The destination should be one related to science or history and would also interest your family.

Use an online site like Map Quest to determine the distance between your house and the destination.

**2.** Research each destination and answer the following questions in the table below.
What could you learn about science or history?
Why would your family enjoy it?
What expenses would be involved?

**3.** Create a budget for each trip.
Create an itemized list with each expense listed: (food, hotel, gas, admission prices).

**4.** After considering the positives and negatives for each location, select the best destination for your family.

**5.** For your parents, create an Animoto presentation (*http://animoto.com/*) that persuasively highlights the educational and interesting parts of the destination. You will also provide them with a budget for the trip. Use the following table to plan your trip.

## Project Options

This assignment could be changed to students planning a school field trip.

| Destination 1: ( miles away) | | | Destination 2: ( miles away) | | |
|---|---|---|---|---|---|
| Learn About Science or History: | | | Learn About Science or History: | | |
| Family Enjoyment: | | | Family Enjoyment: | | |
| Expenses | Calculations | Cost | Expense | Calculations | Cost |
| Adult Admission Price | | | Adult Admission Price | | |
| Youth Admission Price | | | Children's Admission Price | | |
| Food | | | Food | | |
| Gas | | | Gas | | |
| Hotel | | | Hotel | | |
| | | | | | |
| | | | | | |
| Positives: | | | Positives: | | |
| Negatives: | | | Negatives: | | |
| Choice: | | | | | |

## Scoring Rubric

| | 1 | 2 | 3 | 4 |
|---|---|---|---|---|
| Students will create a budget for two educational family trips using their skills of addition, multiplication, and division. | Budget lists a few expenses. Few calculations are correct. | Budget accurately accounts for some of the expenses. Several calculation mistakes. | The budget accurately accounts for a majority of the expenses. One calculation mistake. | The budget accurately accounts for all expenses. All calculations are correct. |
| Students will design a video persuading their family to go on this trip. | The presentation persuasively highlights a few of the positive aspects of the trip. | The presentation persuasively highlights some of the positive aspects of the trip. | The presentation persuasively highlights most of the positive aspects of the trip. | The presentation persuasively highlights all the positive aspects of the trip. |

# Sample Student Work

| | |
|---|---|
| **Destination:**<br>Adventure Science Center<br>(120 miles away) | **Destination:**<br>Mammoth Cave National Park<br>(200 miles away) |
| **Learn About Science:**<br>The science center has lots of hands on activities for kids. There are exhibits about your body, the planets, engineering, and lots more. | **Learn About Science:**<br>At Mammoth Cave we can learn about how caves were formed and how they are changing. We can also explore the nature. There are even packets on the website that have activities for our family to do while we are visiting. |
| **Family Enjoyment:**<br>The kids would like it because there are lots of things to play with. There is even a climbing area for them. | **Family Enjoyment:**<br>Our family can walk the trails and even go bicycling on them. We've never seen such a large cave before so that would be exciting for everyone. There are exhibits within the Visitor's Center that we can see for free. |

| Expense | Calculations | Cost | Expense | Calculations | Cost |
|---|---|---|---|---|---|
| Adult Admission Price | $12 x 2 adults = $24 | $24 | Adult Admission Price | $10 x 2 adults = $20 | $20 |
| Youth Admission Price | $10 x 2 youths = $20 | $20 | Children's Admission Price | $8 x 2 children = $16 | $16 |
| Food | $7 (estimate) x 4 people = $28 per meal

$28 x 4 meals = $112 | $112 | Food | $7 (estimate) x 4 people = $28 per meal

$28 x 4 meals = $112 | $112 |
| Gas | 260 miles (round trip)/Car (25 mpg) = 10.4 gallons of gas

10.4 gallons x $3.50 (per gallon) = $36.40 | $36.40 | Gas | 400 miles (round trip)/ Car (25 mpg) = 16 gallons of gas

16 gallons x $3.50 (per gallon) = $56 | $56 |
| Hotel | Double room $89.99 | $89.99 | Hotel | Double room $71.99 | $71.99 |
| | | | | | |
| | | $282.39 | | | $275.99 |

Positives:
- Nicer hotel with pool
- Lots of kid exhibits

Positives:
- Could take the Frozen Niagara Tour
- A little cheaper
- Could take a hike which would be free
- They have a picnicking area

Negatives:
- A little more expensive
- I-Max theater costs extra
- Fewer fun things for parents

Negatives:
- Farther away

Choice: Mammoth Cave

**Animoto presentation:** *http://animoto.com/play/l0Nvufu0wPJa7UKl1qL0ZQ*

# WHAT IS YOUR OPINION?

## Standards

NUMBERS AND OPERATIONS – FRACTIONS

**4.NF.C.5:** Express a fraction with a denominator 10 as an equivalent fraction with denominator 100, and use this technique to add two fractions with respective denominators 10 and 100.

**4.NF.C.7:** Compare two decimals to hundredths by reasoning about their size. Recognize that comparisons are valid only when the two decimals refer to the same whole. Record the results of comparisons with symbols >, =, <, and justify the conclusions.

## Learning Objective

Students will create and administer a survey to analyze student opinions about a school issue.

## Technology Needed

Student groups will use Google Form to create and administer a survey about a school issue that they select.

- Google Form at Google Docs

    (either the students or the teacher will need a free Google account)

- Portable tablets that have Internet access such as iPod

- Touches, iPads, Kindle, Nook (one per group)

- Two Google Forms Tutorials:

    (Teacher may need to download them before this project if the school blocks the YouTube website.)

    Google Form Tutorial Video: *http://www.youtube.com/watch?v=WMXgutYKMgk*
    Google Form for the classroom: *http://www.youtube.com/watch?v=AeiDxeLVvuQ*

## Project Tasks

Have you ever wondered how polls are done? How did they calculate that 70% of Americans like a certain food or type of car? Do they ask every single person in America? NO, they use a polling percentage or a "sample" (or part of the population). Groups of students in your class will create their own poll, ask students around your school about their opinion on a specific school issue, and then predict the percentage of student opinions about that issue at your school.

## Deciding on a School Issue

1. Your teacher will divide the class into small groups of 2 to 4 students.

2. Your group will discuss issues around your school that you would like opinions from your classmates. Possible school issues could include a new club for your school, a new enrichment class, new playground equipment, what new technology you would like, or new classroom materials your classmates would like.

3. Your group will create a survey in Google Forms. Record the issue that your group decided on the line below:

_____

4. Discuss this issue in your group. Decide on a question and possible choices for this issue and record them below. You should record 4-6 choices.

---

**Example:**

*Issue:* iPad Apps We Should Purchase, our class had a $25 iTunes card donation.

*Survey Question:* What iPad apps do you think we should purchase with our $25?

*Helpful text:* Select your top three choices.

**Choices:**

1. Explain Everything (design and narration tool) – $4.99
2. Docs to Go (Word, Excel, PowerPoint) - $14.95
3. Volcano – $2.99
4. iBiology4Kids - $4.99
5. World Atlas HD – $1.99
6. Quick Graph+ - $1.99
7. GarageBand (to create music) - $4.99

---

Your Group's School or Class Issue: _____

Survey Question: _____

Choice 1: _____

Choice 2: _____

Choice 3: _____

Choice 4: _____

Choice 5: _____

Choice 6: _____

**5.** Show these questions and choice options to your teacher for approval or possible revision.

**6.** Create your survey using Google Form

Learn how to use Google Form by viewing one of the following tutorials:

Google Form Tutorial Video: *http://www.youtube.com/watch?v=WMXgutYKMgk*
Google Form for the classroom: *http://www.youtube.com/watch?v=AeiDxeLVvuQ*

**7.** Your teacher can log into Google Drive for you. Your group will begin to create a new form.

**8.** Create your survey.

   **a.** Type a title for your survey.

   **b.** Type your question.

   **c.** Now for type of question: select "Multiple choice" if you want students to select only one answer and select "Check Box" if you want them to select more than one answer.

   **d.** Click "Done" when finished with this question.

   **e.** You will see "Question Two" after your question. Move your pointer over it and it highlights.

   **f.** Click the image of the Trash Can to the far right of the highlighted area over Question Two.

   **g.** At the bottom of the screen in small letters, you will see the link to your survey. You can try it out! Take your survey several times. Click "Submit another response" between trials.

**9.** Now you can look at your trial results.

   **a.** Return to the Google Drive homepage.

   **b.** Click on "Owned by me" and select the name of your survey.

   **c.** You will see your trial results in a spreadsheet. Click on "Form" just above the spreadsheet and select "Show summary of responses". You will see graphs and percentages of your results.

   **d.** If you are pleased with the type of results or data that you see, then you should delete the trial data from the spreadsheet. Highlight the rows to delete and select "Delete rows" under the Edit menu.

**10.** Decide how you will have 10 other classmates take the survey.

   **a.** The easiest way would be to open the survey on an iPad, iPod Touch, or any other tablet device that is connected to the Internet. Your group will only need one device. It will only take a few seconds for each of your 10 classmates to take your survey question. Click the "Submit another response" before you give it to another student.

   **b.** You could also print 10 copies of your survey question to give to 10 other students. But if you do this, your group will have to type in all 10 responses into Google Forms.

## Give your survey

**11.** Now you are ready to "launch" your survey!
In other words, have classmates complete your survey.

    **a.** Go give the survey to 10 of your classmates! Have fun with it!

    **b.** Check your responses in the Google spreadsheet.

## Working with your results

**12.** Print the results from your survey spreadsheet and the summary graphs.

**13.** Each group will meet and write your responses to the following questions:
How accurate do you think your survey results are? In other words, do you think the survey results really represent or explain what students in your class think about your school issue? Explain.
Calculate the mean, median, and mode for your question.

**14.** How could your group have improved your survey question? Explain.
What conclusions can you draw from your survey results?
Fractions: Put your answers in the table below.

    **a.** Take the results for each option of your survey question and write it as a fraction. For example, if 5 people selected option 1 and 10 classmates took your survey, then your fraction is $\frac{5}{10}$.

    **b.** Now, create an equivalent fraction with a denominator of 100. For example, is equivalent to $\frac{50}{100}$.

    Decimals: (Put your answers in the table below:)
Take each fraction that has the denominator of 100 and convert it to a decimal. For example, $\frac{50}{100}$ equals .50

| Survey Question Options | Results | Fraction with 10 as Denominator | Fraction with 100 as Denominator | Decimal |
|---|---|---|---|---|
|  |  |  |  |  |
|  |  |  |  |  |
|  |  |  |  |  |
|  |  |  |  |  |
|  |  |  |  |  |
|  |  |  |  |  |

## Extensions

**1.** Review the survey and calculations of another group. How accurate do you think their results and analysis are? Explain. What recommendations would you have for this group?

**2.** Do this same survey but gather data from another class at your grade level. Did you get the same results? Explain.

# Scoring Rubric

| Students will create and administer a survey to analyze student opinions about a school issue. | 1 Needs Much Revision | 2 Needs Some Revision | 3 Proficient | 4 Excellent |
|---|---|---|---|---|
| | • Survey questions and options are missing or unrelated to the assigned school issue.<br><br>• Very few students took the survey.<br><br>• Incomplete answers to questions or no response to some questions. Responses not connected to survey results. | • Survey questions and options are missing some important elements.<br><br>• Surveys were given to a few other students but not 10 students in the class.<br><br>• Incomplete answers to questions; Illogical responses. Little connection of conclusions to results. | • Surveys were given to other students; no complaints by students.<br><br>• Adequate answers to question; Logical responses; Connection of conclusions to results. | • Considerable thought and insight in deciding on school issue with no assistance from the teacher.<br><br>• Survey questions and options are comprehensive and perceptive.<br><br>• All students in the group gave surveys to other students; were courteous to others.<br><br>• Comprehensive answers to questions; Logical in-depth responses; Clear connection of conclusions to results. |

# Sample Student Work

## Survey:

Issue: iPad Apps We Should Purchase, our class had a $25 iTunes card donation.

Question 1: What iPad apps do you think we should purchase with our $25?

Helpful text: Select your top three choices.

Choices:

**1.** Explain Everything (design and narration tool) – $4.99

**2.** Docs to Go (Word, Excel, PowerPoint) - $14.95

**3.** Volcano – $2.99

**4.** iBiology4Kids - $4.99

**5.** World Atlas HD – $1.99

**6.** Quick Graph+ - $1.99

**7.** GarageBand (to create music) - $4.99

Print the results from your survey spreadsheet and the summary graphs.

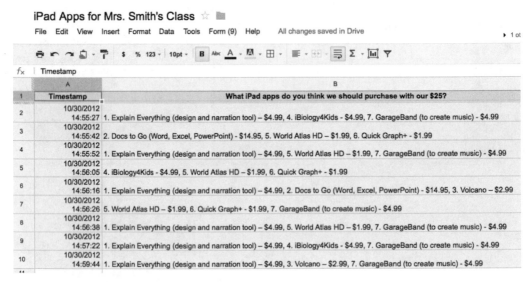

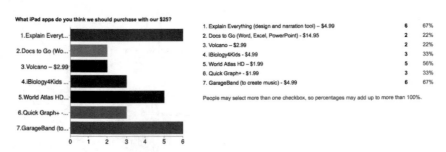

## Survey results

**1.** *How accurate do you think your survey results are? In other words, do you think the survey results really represent or explain what students in your class think about your school issue? Explain.* I think that the results of our survey question are good. I think it shows what people think in our class.

**2.** *Calculate the mean, median, and mode for your question.* Mean = 3.9; Median = 3; Mode is a tie between 2, 3, and 6.

**3.** *How could your group have improved your survey question? Explain.* We could have looked up on the Internet what apps most other 4th grade students like. We could have asked other people in our class what apps they like. We could have asked our librarian and other fourth grade teachers what apps they like. Then we could have made better choices of apps to put in our question.

**4.** *What conclusion(s) can you draw from your survey results?* Explain The three most popular apps were Explain Everything, GarageBand, and World Atlas HD.

| | Survey Question Options | Results | Fraction with 10 as Denominator | Fraction with 100 as Denominator | Decimal |
|---|---|---|---|---|---|
| **1.** | Explain Everything (design and narration tool) – $4.99 | 6 | $\frac{6}{10}$ | $\frac{60}{100}$ | .60 |
| **2.** | Docs to Go (Word, Excel, PowerPoint) - $14.95 | 2 | $\frac{2}{10}$ | $\frac{20}{100}$ | .20 |
| **3.** | Volcano – $2.99 | 2 | $\frac{2}{10}$ | $\frac{20}{100}$ | .20 |
| **4.** | iBiology4Kids - $4.99 | 3 | $\frac{3}{10}$ | $\frac{30}{100}$ | .30 |
| **5.** | World Atlas HD – $1.99 | 5 | $\frac{5}{10}$ | $\frac{50}{100}$ | .50 |
| **6.** | Quick Graph+ - $1.99 | 3 | $\frac{3}{10}$ | $\frac{30}{100}$ | .30 |
| **7.** | GarageBand (to create music) - $4.99 | 6 | $\frac{6}{10}$ | $\frac{60}{100}$ | .60 |

# WHAT IS THE BEST BREAKFAST CEREAL?

## Standards

### OPERATIONS & ALGEBRAIC THINKING

**4.OA.A.1** Interpret a multiplication equation as a comparison, e.g., interpret $35 = 5 \times 7$ as a statement that 35 is 5 times as many as 7 and 7 times as many as 5. Represent verbal statements of multiplicative comparisons as multiplication equations.

**4.OA.A.2** Multiply or divide to solve word problems involving multiplicative comparison, e.g., by using drawings and equations with a symbol for the unknown number to represent the problem, distinguishing multiplicative comparison from additive comparison.

**4.OA.A.3** Solve multistep word problems posed with whole numbers and having whole-number answers using the four operations, including problems in which remainders must be interpreted. Represent these problems using equations with a letter standing for the unknown quantity. Assess the reasonableness of answers using mental computation and estimation strategies including rounding.

### MEASUREMENT & DATA

**4.MD.A.2** Use the four operations to solve word problems involving distances, intervals of time, liquid volumes, masses of objects, and money, including problems involving simple fractions or decimals, and problems that require expressing measurements given in a larger unit in terms of a smaller unit. Represent measurement quantities using diagrams such as number line diagrams that feature a measurement scale.

## Learning Objective

Students will use a spreadsheet to perform multiple calculations to determine the best cereal based on multiple factors.

## Resources needed

- Computer with Internet access
- Spreadsheet software such as Microsoft Excel
- Real Cereal, purchase cereal for students to taste

# What is the BEST Breakfast Cereal?

Almost everyone eats breakfast cereal whether you eat it in the morning or later in the day. Have you noticed how many types of cereal there are in your local grocery story? There is a great variation in costs, how they are packaged, their taste, and nutritional value. Your teacher will divide the class into pairs to work on this project.

## Project Tasks

*Let's go to the grocery store.*

1. Each group will discuss and write down the names of 10 breakfast cereals that you like or have eaten before.

2. Go to the grocery store or research online to gather information and prices about those 10 cereals.

3. Use the table below to record the cereal name, size of box (in ounces), and price.

| | Cereal Name | Size (in ounces) | Price (in Cents Per Ounce) |
|---|---|---|---|
| 1. | | | |
| 2. | | | |
| 3. | | | |
| 4. | | | |
| 5. | | | |
| 6. | | | |
| 7. | | | |
| 8. | | | |
| 9. | | | |
| 10. | | | |

# Using the spreadsheet

**4.** Add the data from your chart to a spreadsheet.

**5.** Add another column called "Price in Cents/Ounce per oz", another column called "Taste Index", and another column called "Adjusted Worth per oz".

**6.** How would you calculate the cost of each cereal per ounce? Enter this formula into the cell for the first cereal under the "Price in Cents/Ounce per oz" column. The spreadsheet will display the result of the formula. Use the Fill Down feature to copy the formula down to display the cost per ounce for the other 9 cereals. Remember that lower prices per ounce are better.

**7.** So how much do you like the taste this cereal? Your teacher will provide a small sample of each cereal. Assign each cereal a "taste index" which is a value from 1 to 5. A rating of 1 is "best taste". A rating of 5 is "worst taste". Record these indexes in your spreadsheet. This is your personal opinion for how much you like the taste of the cereal. Record this taste rating for each cereal on your spreadsheet in the "Taste Index" column. Remember that the lower the taste index numbers are better.

**8.** In the cell for the first cereal under the "Adjusted Worth" column, create a formula that adds the "Price in Cents/Ounce per oz" and "Taste Index". Use the Fill Down feature to copy the formula down to display the adjusted worth for the other 9 cereals.

Here is a sample spreadsheet:

| | A | B | C | D | E | F |
|---|---|---|---|---|---|---|
| 1 | What is the BEST Breakfast Cereal? | | | | | |
| 2 | | | | | | |
| 3 | | | | Price in | | Adjusted Worth |
| 4 | Cereal | Size (in oz*) | Price | Cents per oz | Taste Index | Per oz |
| 5 | Honey Bunches Oats/Almonds | 14.5 | $2.58 | 17.8 | 3 | 9.0 |
| 6 | Cocoa Krispies | 16.5 | $3.00 | 18.2 | 1 | 5.1 |
| 7 | Honey Nut Cheerios | 17 | $3.58 | 21.1 | 2 | 8.2 |
| 8 | Cap'n Crunch, Peanut Butter | 12.5 | $2.54 | 20.3 | 2 | 5.8 |
| 9 | Lucky Charms | 11.5 | $2.98 | 25.9 | 2 | 7.9 |
| 10 | Frosted Flakes, Chocolate | 14.7 | $2.98 | 20.3 | 3 | 9.1 |
| 11 | Froot Loops | 17 | $3.36 | 19.8 | 1 | 5.3 |
| 12 | Honey Smacks | 15.3 | $2.98 | 19.5 | 1 | 5.1 |
| 13 | Raisin Bran, double scoop raisins | 23.5 | $3.50 | 14.9 | 5 | 13.9 |
| 14 | Special K | 18 | $3.88 | 21.6 | 3 | 10.1 |
| 15 | | | | | | |
| 16 | | Averages | $3.14 | 19.9 | 2 | 8 |
| 17 | * oz means ounces | | | | | |
| 18 | | | | | | |

9. Class Discussion: From your calculations, which is the best cereal or the cereal with the lowest Adjusted Worth? Is this the cereal that you thought would be the best cereal? Explain why or why not.

10. Class Discussion: Are there other factors that may help to determine which is the best cereal? What might they be? Explain.

11. Add the Fullness Factor, Nutrition Data Factor, and Completeness Score to your spreadsheet.

Here is a sample spreadsheet:

| | A | B | C | D | E | F | G | H | I | J |
|---|---|---|---|---|---|---|---|---|---|---|
| 1 | What is the BEST Breakfast Cereal? | | | | | | | | | |
| 2 | | | | | | | | | | |
| 3 | | | | Price in | | | Adjusted Worth | | Fullness | Nutrition Data | Completeness |
| 4 | Cereal | Size (in oz*) | Price | Cents per oz | Taste Index | Per oz | | Factor (1-5) | (1-5) | Score; 1-100 |
| 5 | Honey Bunches Oats/Almonds | 14.5 | $2.58 | 17.8 | 3 | 9.0 | | 1.7 | 3 | 49.0 |
| 6 | Cocoa Krispies | 16.5 | $3.00 | 18.2 | 1 | 5.1 | | 1.5 | 3.1 | 59.0 |
| 7 | Honey Nut Cheerios | 17 | $3.58 | 21.1 | 2 | 8.2 | | 1.9 | 4.2 | 78.0 |
| 8 | Cap'n Crunch, Peanut Butter | 12.5 | $2.54 | 20.3 | 2 | 5.8 | | 1.6 | 1.8 | 38.0 |
| 9 | Lucky Charms | 11.5 | $2.98 | 25.9 | 2 | 7.9 | | 1.6 | 3.9 | 71.0 |
| 10 | Frosted Flakes, Chocolate | 14.7 | $2.98 | 20.3 | 3 | 9.1 | | 1.5 | 3.1 | 51.0 |
| 11 | Froot Loops | 17 | $3.36 | 19.8 | 1 | 5.3 | | 1.4 | 3.3 | 56.0 |
| 12 | Honey Smacks | 15.3 | $2.98 | 19.5 | 1 | 5.1 | | 1.6 | 3.1 | 55.0 |
| 13 | Raisin Bran, double scoop raisins | 23.5 | $3.50 | 14.9 | 5 | 13.9 | | 1.9 | 3.9 | 71.0 |
| 14 | Special K | 18 | $3.88 | 21.6 | 3 | 10.1 | | 2.2 | 4.1 | 68.0 |
| 15 | | | | | | | | | | |
| 16 | | Averages | $3.14 | 19.9 | 2 | 8 | | 1.7 | 3.4 | 60 |
| 17 | * oz means ounces | | | | | | | | | |
| 18 | | | | | | | | | | |

## 12. Group Discussion

Write the answers to the following questions.

**a.** Which 3 cereals make you feel more full?

**b.** Which 3 cereals are the most nutritious?

**c.** Which 3 cereals have the highest Completeness Score?

**d.** Are the 3 cereals the same on the above questions? Explain.

**e.** Discuss the BEST cereal using the cost, taste, fullness, nutrition, and completeness of nutrition factors in your discussion.

## 13. Class Discussion

**a.** Groups will present their findings and conclusions about the BEST cereal.

**b.** We will have a class discussion about the most important factors are in deciding what factors (cost, taste, fullness, nutrition, and completeness) of nutrition factors are the most important in deciding on the BEST cereal.

## Scoring Rubric

| | 1 Needs Much Revision | 2 Needs Some Revision | 3 Proficient | 4 Excellent |
|---|---|---|---|---|
| **Students will use a spreadsheet to perform multiple calculations to determine the best cereal based on multiple factors.** | Most formulas and calculations are not correct even with assistance from teacher.<br><br>Students in groups did not decide upon the BEST cereal. Conclusions are very short, incomplete, and illogical. | Some formulas and calculations are not correct even with assistance from teacher.<br><br>Students in groups selected the BEST cereal and wrote conclusions using 1-2 of the 5 factors from this project. Conclusions may be incomplete or illogical. | All formulas and calculations are correct with some assistance from teacher.<br><br>Students in groups selected the BEST cereal and wrote adequate conclusions using at least 3 of the 5 factors from this project. | All formulas and calculations are correct on the first attempt with no assistance.<br><br>Students in groups selected the BEST cereal and wrote excellent, logical, conclusions using at least 4 of the 5 factors from this project. |

# 14. Extensions

Use the *http://nutritiondata.self.com* website to look up the Fullness Factor, Nutrition Data Factor, and Completeness Score for each cereal. The following explains these terms.

a. The **Fullness Factor™ (FF)** rates foods on a 0 to 5 scale that predicts the fullness effect of the food. Higher FF numbers indicate that a food is more filling or satisfying per calorie. Lower FF numbers suggest that a food will supply a lot of calories before you feel full. Therefore, foods with high FF numbers may support weight loss and foods with low FF numbers may support weight gain.

b. The **ND (Nutrition Data) Rating** scores foods on a 0 to 5 scale based on the FDA recommendations for a healthy diet. A higher ND Rating indicates that a food is more nutritious. The formula used to create the ND Rating takes into account the nutrient density of the food (how many nutrients per calorie), how many different essential nutrients are present, the relative importance of the nutrients present, and the amount of nutrients that are frequently overconsumed, such as sodium, cholesterol, and saturated fat.

c. **Completeness Score** (range 1-100): Very few foods contain a complete array of essential nutrients; therefore, it's important to eat a variety of foods to fulfill our nutritional needs. This Nutrient Balance Indicator™ lets you see at a glance the nutritional strengths and weaknesses of a food, and can help you construct meals that are more nutritionally balanced.

Each spoke in the wheel represents a different nutrient. The spoke for dietary fiber is colored green, protein is blue, vitamins are purple, minerals are white, and yellow represents a group of commonly overconsumed nutrients—saturated fat, cholesterol, and sodium. The density of each nutrient is indicated by how far that spoke extends towards the edge of the graph. A Completeness Score™ between 0 and 100 summarizes how complete the food is with respect to 23 essential nutrients.

**15.** If you were working for a cereal company, and you were conducting a consumer survey of your cereal for the purpose of improving your cereal, what five questions would you ask?

**16.** Add specific nutrition data to your spreadsheet to include fat, sugars, protein, and dietary fiber for each cereal.

    **a.** Create a Nutrition Index that subtracts the good nutrition from the bad nutrition. The lower numbers are best.

    **b.** Create an Adjusted Value by adding the Taste Index and Nutrition Index.

    **c.** Create an Adjusted Worth by adding Cost + Taste Index + Nutrition Index.

    **d.** Which is a better indicator of the best cereal? Why?

    **e.** Add a Calories column. How can this contribute to the Value or Worth of a cereal?

Here is a sample spreadsheet:

### What is the BEST Breakfast Cereal?

| Cereal | Size (in oz*) | Price | Price in Cents per oz | Cost in cents for 1 c. or 3.5 oz | Taste Index | Nutrition Index | Adjusted Value Taste + Nutrition | Adjusted Worth Cost+Taste+Nutrition | Bad Fat | Bad Sugars | Good Protein | Good Fiber | Serving Size in cups | Convert to ounces | Scale Factor | Bad Fat | Bad Carbs | Good Protein | Good Fiber | Calories w/o* milk |
|---|---|---|---|---|---|---|---|---|---|---|---|---|---|---|---|---|---|---|---|---|
| Honey Bunches Oats/Almonds | 14.5 | $2.58 | 17.8 | 62.3 | 3 | 6.7 | 9.7 | 68.3 | 3 | 6 | 2 | 2 | 0.75 | 2.6 | 1.3 | 4.0 | 8.1 | 2.7 | 2.7 | 130 |
| Cocoa Krispies | 16.5 | $3.00 | 18.2 | 63.6 | 1 | 13.5 | 14.5 | 65.6 | 3.5 | 12 | 2 | 0 | 1.00 | 3.5 | 1.0 | 3.5 | 12.0 | 2.0 | 0.0 | 120 |
| Honey Nut Cheerios | 17 | $3.58 | 21.1 | 73.7 | 2 | 7.8 | 9.8 | 77.7 | 2 | 9 | 3 | 2 | 0.75 | 2.6 | 1.3 | 2.6 | 11.7 | 3.9 | 2.6 | 110 |
| Cap'n Crunch, Peanut Butter | 12.5 | $2.54 | 20.3 | 71.1 | 2 | 11.1 | 13.1 | 75.1 | 2.5 | 9 | 2 | 1 | 0.75 | 2.6 | 1.3 | 3.3 | 11.7 | 2.6 | 1.3 | 110 |
| Lucky Charms | 11.5 | $2.98 | 25.9 | 90.7 | 2 | 11.2 | 13.2 | 94.7 | 1.3 | 14 | 2.5 | 1.6 | 1.00 | 3.5 | 1.0 | 1.3 | 14.0 | 2.5 | 1.6 | 142 |
| Frosted Flakes, Chocolate | 14.7 | $2.98 | 20.3 | 71.0 | 3 | 15.6 | 18.6 | 77.0 | 1 | 13 | 1 | 1 | 0.75 | 2.6 | 1.3 | 1.3 | 16.9 | 1.3 | 1.3 | 120 |
| Froot Loops | 17 | $3.36 | 19.8 | 69.2 | 1 | 9.0 | 10.0 | 71.2 | 1 | 12 | 1 | 3 | 1.00 | 3.5 | 1.0 | 1.0 | 12.0 | 1.0 | 3.0 | 110 |
| Honey Smacks | 15.3 | $2.98 | 19.5 | 68.2 | 1 | 16.3 | 17.3 | 70.2 | 0.5 | 15 | 2 | 1 | 0.75 | 2.6 | 1.3 | 0.7 | 19.5 | 2.6 | 1.3 | 100 |
| Raisin Bran, double scoop raisins | 23.5 | $3.50 | 14.9 | 52.1 | 5 | 6.0 | 11.0 | 62.1 | 1 | 16 | 5 | 6 | 1.00 | 3.5 | 1.0 | 1.0 | 16.0 | 5.0 | 6.0 | 180 |
| Special K | 18 | $3.88 | 21.6 | 75.4 | 3 | -3.5 | -0.5 | 81.4 | 0.5 | 4 | 7 | 1 | 1.00 | 3.5 | 1.0 | 0.5 | 4.0 | 7.0 | 1.0 | 117 |
| Average | | $3.14 | 19.9 | 70 | 2 | 9 | 12 | 74 | | | | | | | | | | | | 124 |

* oz means ounces
*w/o means without
* 1 cup of dry cereal = 3.5 ounces

# ANSWER KEY
## PRE/POST ASSESSMENT
## DOMAIN 1

### 4.OA.A.1
1. 8 x n = 64; n = 8 (64 ÷ 8 = n; n = 8)
2. 72 is __9__ times as many as 8 and 8 times as many as 9 (72 ÷ 8 = 9; 72 ÷ 9 = 8)

### 4.OA.A.2
1. 29 x 3 = 87 points
2. Priya has $30.00 and Raul has $5.00 (Priya - $10 x 3 = $30 and Raul $10 ÷ 2 = $5)

### 4.OA.A.3
1. 13 x 8 = 104; 48 x 2 = 96; 104 – 96 = 8 pieces left over
2. Toby needs to earn an additional $13.00. He has earned $20 allowance ($5 x 4 weeks = $20); He has earned $42 for yard work ($7 x 6 hours = $42), earning a total of $62 ($20 + $42 = $62). He needs $75 for the skateboard: $75 - $62 = $13 left to earn.

### 4.OA.B.4
1. Answer: 1 x 12, 2 x 6, 3 x 4, 4 x 3, 6 x 2, and 12 x 1; explanations will vary, but should address finding factors.
2. Answer: An "X" should be placed on the following numbers:

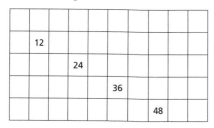

### 4.OA.C.5
1. 1350 pennies. The rule is to triple the previous number of pennies. (450 x 3 = 1350)
2. Pattern: add 15 minutes

| 3:00 | 3:15 | 3:30 | 3:45 | 4:00 | 4:15 |

### ANSWER KEY 4.OA.A.1
1. 5 x 3 = 15 pieces of bubblegum
2. 5 x 2 = 10 minutes
3. 16 = 4 x n; n = 4 yards or 16 ÷ 4 = n; n = 4 times more yards
4. 3 x 4 = 12 books read
5. 5 x _4__ = 20, so it is 4 times longer. Related division problem: 20 ÷ 5 = 4

### ANSWER KEY 4.OA.A.2
1. $810 / 9 = $90
2. Mike scored 14 x 3 = 42 points. John scored 23 x 2 = 46 points. Since 42 is less than 46, John scored more points.
3. (42 x 6) + (54 x 4) = 252 + 216 = 468 photos
4. 2 x $3.50 = $7.00; 2 x $2.50 = $5.00; $5.00 + $7.00 = $12.00 total. Raul and his sister will need to have $12.00 to buy two slices of pizza and two bottles of water.
5. 12 + 15 = 27 children in the class. 27 children x 7 pieces of candy each =189 pieces of candy

### ANSWER KEY 4.OA.B.3
1. 24 + 52 + 77 = 153;  153 ÷ 3 = 51
2. (25 x n) + z = 83; (25 x 3) + 8 = 83. He will need 4 boxes.
3. 5 x 12 = 60 cookies; 60 divided by 8 equals 7 with remainder of 4. There are 4 cookies left over.
4. 16 + 12 + 7 = 35 coats. 35 ÷ 5 = 7 coats per team member.
5. 145 + 127 + 99 = 371; 500 – 371 = 129 bars of candy left in the store.

### ANSWER KEY 4.OA.B.4
A. Top left corner: 9x2and 2x9; middle region 3x6 and 6x3; bottom region 1x18 and 18x1

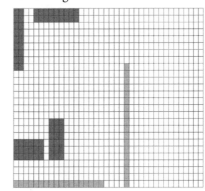

b. 1, 2, 3, 6, 9, 18 (Arrays should reflect these factors)
2.   5 + 2 + 2 + 2 + 5 = 16 (19 and 47 are prime numbers – the others are composite)
3. c. Explanations may include divisibility rule of 6, counting by 6
4. a. 5, 10, 15, 20, 25, 30, 35, 40, 45, 50, 55, 60, 65, 70, 75, 80, 85, 90, 95, 100

b. If the multiple ends in 5 or 0 in the one's digit/position.
5. Circle 5, 7, 11, 13, 17, 19; Underline 6, 8, 9, 10, 12, 14, 15, 16, 18, 20

### ANSWER KEY 4.OA.C.5
1. 11, 16, 22.
The pattern is +1, +2, +3, +4, +5, +6
2. The rule is to add three.

| IN | OUT |
|----|-----|
| 6  | 9   |
| 15 | 18  |
| **29** | 32 |
| 56 | **59** |
| 62 | **65** |
| **72** | 75 |

3.

4. 32 Rule: double the number
5.

| 1  | 3  |
|----|----|
| 4  | 9  |
| 7  | 15 |
| 10 | 21 |
| 12 | 25 |

Rule: double the first number and add one.

# ANSWER KEY
## PRE/POST ASSESSMENT
## DOMAIN 2 NBT

### 4.NBT.A.1
1. a. 57 hundreds = 570 tens
   b. 830 tens = 83 hundreds
2. a. 500 ÷ 5 = 100
   b. 50 ÷ 5 = 10
Answers will vary, but should include that the value of the digit depends on its placement in a multi-digit number. For example, the value of a digit in the ten's place is ten times that of a digit in the one's place.

### 4.NBT.A.2
1. 97,246 = 90,000 + 7,000 + 200+ 40 + 6
2. 1,892 < 1,981

## 4.NBT.A.3
1. $800 + 900 + 800 = 2,500$ soda can tabs
2. $\$1,500.00 - \$400 = \$1,100.00$

## 4.NBT.B.4
1. $35 - n = 6$;  $n = 29$
2. $1,845 + 1,762 = 3,607$ points

## 4.NBT.B.5
1. $175 \times 12 = 2,100$ pounds
2. $1,395 \times 7 = 9,765$ gallons of water

## 4.NBT.B.6
1. $275 \div 5 = 55$. Students should show how they solved the problem (answers will vary).
2. $1,250 \div 8 = 156$ flower boxes; Yes, there will be 2 nails left over

## ANSWER KEY 4.NBT.A.1
1. $4,000 = 40$ hundreds
2. $n = 700 \div 10$; $n = 70$. Steven has 70 baseball cards.
3. Christopher thought he had $80. $n = \$80 \times 10$
4. c. 720,000 is ten times 72,000 $(72,000 \times 10 = 720,000)$
5. Thomas is correct. Jeannie has 10 times as many songs. Explanations will vary but should include that ten times 200 is 2,000. 20,000 is 100 times 200

## ANSWER KEY 4.NBT.A.2
1. a. $7,000,000 + 40,000 + 200 + 9$.
   b. seven million forty thousand two hundred nine
   c.  <
   d. 9,307,090
2. 975,220; Nine hundred seventy-five thousand, two hundred twenty; $900,000 + 70,000 + 5,000 + 200 + 20$

## ANSWER KEY 4.NBT.A.3
1. a. 6,924,610
   b. 6,924,600
   c. 6,925,000
   d. 6,920,000
   e. 6,900,000
   f. 7,000,000
2. Explanation should include a basic understanding of place value and rounding.
   a. 436,300
   b. 436,000
   c. 400,000
3. 57,000

## ANSWER KEY 4.NBT.B.4
1. Mallory was correct. $22,302 + 2,922 = 25,224$

$$\begin{array}{r} 1\phantom{0000} \\ 22,302 \\ +\ 2,922 \\ \hline 2\,5,2\,2\,4 \end{array}$$

Molly may not have regrouped her 1000s correctly.
2. $2,459 + 2,521 + 3,733 = 8,713$ pennies
3. $5,302 - 1,293 = 4,009$ books
4. $\$180 - (\$34.00 + 29.90 + 52.39) = \$63.71$
5. $1,079 + 75 = 1,154$ baseball cards

## ANSWER KEY 4.NBT.B.5
1. Margaret collected $170.00. ($85 \times \$2.00 = \$170.00$).
Strategy: multiply the number of candy bars sold (85) times the cost of each candy bar ($2.00).
2. The largest number possible is $72 \times 53 = 7,816$
3. $12 \times 24 = 288$ donuts
4. $327 \times 5 = 1,635$ miles
5. $48 \times 60 = 2,880$ seats

## ANSWER KEY 4.NBT.B.6
1. $351 \div 3 = 117$ cans
2. Four dozen cookies is 48 cookies ($12 \times 4 = 48$). There are a total of 5 girls; if each girl receives an equal share, then $48 \div 5 = 9$ cookies each; there will be 3 cookies left over.
3. $125 \div 5 = 25$ students. $25 \times 5 = 125$
4. a. Divide 120 inches by 9 inches = 13 hair bows
b. If you divide 1,625 inches by 9 inches, you get 180 with a remainder of 5. There would be 5 inches left over.

# ANSWER KEY
## PRE/POST ASSESSMENT
## DOMAIN 3 NF

## 4.NF.A.1
1. Answers may vary but equivalent to $\frac{2}{3}$. (Examples: $\frac{4}{6}, \frac{6}{9}, \frac{8}{12}$)
2. c. $\frac{6}{8}$

## 4.NF.A.2
1. a.  <
   b.  >
   c.  =
   d.  >
2. d. $\frac{13}{15}$ ($\frac{4}{5} = \frac{12}{15}$, which is less than $\frac{13}{15}$)

## 4.NF.B.3
1. $3\frac{3}{5}$
2. Amy is correct. The denominator does not change when you add fractions with the same denominator. Models will differ, but show same size parts.

## 4.NF.B.4
1. Yes. She has $4 \times \frac{3}{4} = \frac{12}{4}$ pieces.
2. $\frac{1}{2} \times 22 = 11$ bananas

## 4.NF.C.5
1. $\frac{90}{100}$
2. $\frac{30}{100} + \frac{60}{100} = \frac{90}{100}$

## 4.NF.C.6
1. a. $\frac{10}{100}, \frac{30}{100}, \frac{60}{100}, \frac{70}{100}$
   b. 0.40, 0.80, 0.90
2. Answer: b. $\frac{3}{4} = .75$

## 4.NF.C.7
1. a.  <
   b.  =
   c.  =
2. Answers will vary, but must be less than .45. (Examples: .20, .15, .30, .40). Explanations will vary but should include reference to place value of decimals (the further from zero, the lower the value).

## ANSWER KEY 4.NF.A.1
1. $\frac{4}{8}$
2. Answers will vary, but should be an equivalent fraction for $\frac{1}{3}$ (e.g. $\frac{2}{6}, \frac{3}{9}, \frac{4}{12}$)
3. The girls saved the same amount of bubblegum. $\frac{3}{4} = \frac{6}{8}$
4. a. $\frac{1}{2}$     b. $\frac{2}{4}$     c. $\frac{3}{6}$
5. Answers may vary, but divided into equal parts and shaded to represent $\frac{1}{4}$. (e.g $\frac{2}{8}, \frac{3}{12}, \frac{4}{16}$)

## ANSWER KEY 4.NF.A.2
1. The first and last pictures should be circled ( $\frac{2}{4} = \frac{1}{2}$ and $\frac{5}{10} = \frac{1}{2}$ )
2. $\frac{1}{2}, \frac{2}{3}, \frac{5}{6}$
3. No, $\frac{7}{8}$ is larger than $\frac{7}{12}$ because the smaller the denominator the larger each part of the whole, as it is broken into smaller parts.
4. Josie ate more. Answers may vary, but should include the fact that the pieces must be the same size (common denominator of 8) when comparing, and $\frac{6}{8}$ is greater than $\frac{5}{8}$.

5. Answers may vary but should contain a denominator that is divisible by both 4 and 5. Answers could include $\frac{15}{20}$ and $\frac{16}{20}$ or $\frac{30}{40}$ and $\frac{32}{40}$.

## ANSWER KEY 4.NF.B.3

1. Charles has $\frac{3}{8}$ of the pizza left.

$\frac{3}{8} + \frac{2}{8} = \frac{5}{8}$ *and* $\frac{8}{8}$ (the whole) $- \frac{5}{8} = \frac{3}{8}$

2. Answers will vary, but could include one or more of the following:

$1 + 1 + \frac{1}{2}$ *or* $1 + \frac{1}{2} + \frac{1}{2}$ *or* $\frac{1}{2} + \frac{1}{2} + \frac{1}{2} + \frac{1}{2} + \frac{1}{2}$

3. She will need $3\frac{3}{4}$ cups of flour ($2\frac{1}{4} + 1\frac{2}{4} = 3\frac{3}{4}$)

4. Molly feeds her cat $\frac{2}{3}$ cup of food each day.

5. No, she did not eat $\frac{2}{4}$ of the brownies. Even if the pieces were the same size, she would have eaten 2 out a total of 8 pieces, which would be $\frac{2}{8}$ or $\frac{1}{4}$ of the brownies.

6. Answers may vary but could include: $\frac{1}{8} + \frac{1}{8} + \frac{1}{8} + \frac{1}{8} + \frac{1}{8} + \frac{1}{8} + \frac{1}{8} = \frac{7}{8}$ *or*

$\frac{1}{8} + \frac{1}{8} + \frac{5}{8} = \frac{7}{8}$ *or* $\frac{4}{8} + \frac{3}{8} = \frac{7}{8}$

## ANSWER KEY 4.NF.B.4

1. $4 \times \frac{1}{3} = 1\frac{1}{3}$ (mixed number) or $\frac{4}{3}$ (improper fraction). The model should show two models divided into three equal parts. The first model should have all 3 parts shaded; the second model should have one of the three parts shaded.

2. Yes. $\frac{1}{2} \times 7 = \frac{7}{2} = 3\frac{1}{2}$ hours total

3. $\frac{3}{4} \times 7 = \frac{21}{4} = 5\frac{1}{4}$ hours each week

4. $\frac{4}{5} = \frac{1}{5} + \frac{1}{5} + \frac{1}{5} + \frac{1}{5}$ *or* $\frac{4}{5} = 4 \times \frac{1}{5}$

5. $\frac{3}{4} \times 5 = \frac{15}{4}$ cups or $3\frac{3}{4}$ cups. She will need to buy 2 bags.

## ANSWER KEY 4.NF.C.5

1. $\frac{3}{10} + \frac{60}{100} = \frac{30}{100} + \frac{60}{100} = \frac{90}{100}$ *or* $\frac{9}{10}$

2. $\frac{2}{10} = \frac{20}{100}$

3. $\frac{3}{10} + \frac{40}{100} = \frac{30}{100} + \frac{40}{100} = \frac{70}{100}$ *or* $\frac{7}{10}$ of the garden has been weeded.

4. $\frac{7}{10} = \frac{70}{100}$

5. $\$6 + 9 = \$15$

## ANSWER KEY 4.NF.C.6

1. 0.75 mile

2.

3. $\frac{55}{100}$ inch

4. $\frac{95}{100}$

5. 0.73

## ANSWER KEY 4.NF.C.7

1. 0.03   0.30      0.33      0.40

2. 0.24 < 0.42

   0.40 = 0.4

   1.33 > 0.75

3. Satcha hiked farther. 5.25 miles is farther than 4.95 miles (the whole number has the greatest value in this problem, and five is greater than four).

4. c. Nine tenths is equal to 90 hundredths, which is greater than 67 hundredths.

5. <

# ANSWER KEY
## PRE/POST ASSESSMENT
## DOMAIN 4 MD

### 4.MD.A.1

1. 4 tablespoons = 12 teaspoons (each tablespoon = 3 teaspoons; 4 x 3 = 12)

2. $2\frac{1}{2}$ Hours = 150 minutes (each hour = 60 minutes; 2 x 60 + 30 = 150)

### 4.MD.A.2

1. Austin's baby brother is 4 days older than Ellie's baby brother.
Austin's baby brother is 403 days old (one year has 365 days; one week has 7 days, so 5 weeks = 35 days; + 3 days = 365 days + 35 days + 3 days = 403 days old); 403 – 399 = 4 days

2. Nancy Ann lives closer.
Matthew lives $2\frac{1}{4}$ miles away from school, which is 2.25 miles. Nancy lives 2.2 miles away, which is less than 2.25 miles.

### 4.MD.A.3

1. 10 x 8 = 80 square feet;
   80 x $7.00 = $560.00

2. The dimensions of Caroline's pencil box are 5 centimeters by 10 centimeters.

### 4.MD.B.4

1. $\frac{6}{20}$ of the students like birds and hamsters

2.

### 4.MD.C.5

1. 180 degrees

2. The pie is cut into 60 degree angles

### 4.MD.C.6

1. 140 degrees.

2. Students' angles should measure 70 degrees.

### 4.MD.C.7

1. 45 degrees (A right angle is 90 degrees; 90 degrees ÷2 = 45 degrees).

2. 70 degrees (each slice of pizza is 35 degrees, and each girl ate two slices – 35 degrees x 2 = 70 degrees).

## ANSWER KEY 4.MD.A.1

1. 200 cm (1 meter = 100 cm; 2x100 = 200 cm)

2. 5 ft=60 in; 18 ft=6 yd; 2 yd=72 in; 20 ft=240 in; 36 in=1 yd

3. a. 420 (1 hr=60 min; 60x7=420)

4. 160 oz (1 lb=16 oz; 16x10=160)

5. Hannah's mom is taller because 5 feet 4 inches = 64 inches (5 x 12 = 60; 60 + 4 = 64), and 64 inches is greater than 55 inches.

## ANSWER KEY 4.MD.A.2

1. Ann Marie lives .05 mile closer. ($4\frac{3}{4}$ = 4.75, and 4.75 – 4.7 = 0.05 mile).

2. 3 quarts + 4 quarts = 7 quarts

3. Janice will make $385 in 7 weekends, since $55 x 7 = $385.

4. 12.2 – 10.9 = 1.3 lbs.

5. One gallon = 4 quarts; 4 x 4 = 16 quarts; One gallon = 16 cups; 4 x 16 = 64 cups

## ANSWER KEY 4.MD.A.3

1. A = 91m2 (13m x 7m = 91m2)
P = 40m (13m+13m+7m+7m = 40m)

2. The perimeter of Janae's room is 50 feet (10 + 10 + 15 + 15 = 50 feet). Each roll will cover 10 feet. Divide the total number of feet (50) by the number of feet in each roll (10) to determine the number of rolls needed. 50 ÷ 10 = 5 rolls

3. 242 yards will be needed. (46x2) + (75x2) = 242
4. 750 ft² (110 = 25+25+30+30; 25x30=750)
5. Area = 49 square feet (7 x 7 = 49 square feet); Perimeter = 28 feet (7 + 7 + 7 + 7 = 28 feet)

## ANSWER KEY 4.MD.B.4
1. 13/23 of the students read 4 or more books.
2. b. One read 1 book and one read 9 books.
3.
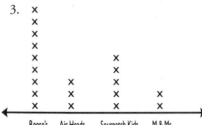

4. a. 5/10 bushel + 5/10 bushel + 5/10 bushel + 5/10 bushel + 5/10 bushel = 25/10 bushels; 25/10 = 2 5/10 = 2 ½ bushels
   b. 4/10 bushel + 4/10 bushel + 4/10 bushel + 4/10 bushel + 4/10 bushel + 4/10 bushel = 24/10 bushels; 24/10 = 2 4/10 = 2 2/5 bushels; 6/10 bushel + 6/10 bushel + 6/10 bushel + 6/10 bushel + 6/10 bushel + 6/10 bushel = 36/10; 36/10 = 3 6/10 = 3 3/5 bushels; 3 3/5 − 2 2/5 = 1 1/5 bushels is the total amount more eaten by the horses that ate 6/10 bushel.

5.

## ANSWER KEY 4.MD.C.5
1. 75/360 or 15/72 or 5/24 or another equivalent fraction
2. Answers may vary, but must represent 90º. (Example: 3:00, 9:00)
3. c
4. a. ray  b. line  c. line segment
5. 55 degrees

## ANSWER KEY 4.MD.C.6
1. 70º
2. a
3. Angle should measure 105º.

---

4. 120º
5. Jimmy is looking at the supplementary angle. (Two angles are supplementary if the sum of both angles equals 180 degrees, which is a straight line.)

## ANSWER KEY 4.MD.C.7
1. 140º
2. Answers will vary, but the sum of the angles should be 90º.
3. 120º + 120º + 120º = 360º
4. 90º – The minute hand is pointing to the 12 at 7:00. After 15 minutes, the minute hand is pointing to 3. The minute hand has moved 90º (It has moved 1/4 of a circle; a circle is 360º, and 360 ÷ 4 = 90º).
5. 25º (800º − 550º = 250º).

# ANSWER KEY
## PRE/POST ASSESSMENT
## DOMAIN 5 G

### 4.G.A.1
1. Answers will vary, but the figure should contain both perpendicular and parallel lines. An example could be

Opposite sides are parallel.
Adjoining sides are perpendicular.
Another could be:

Left and right sides are parallel. Left and right sides are perpendicular to the bottom side.
2. Line segment, because it has a starting point and ending point.

### 4.G.A.2
1. Right triangle (it contains a 90 degree angle).
2. Zero. The angles are all acute (less than 90 degrees). An obtuse angle is greater than 90 degrees.

### 4.G.A.3
1. The following figures should be circled:

2. Answers will vary, but the shape should have no lines of symmetry.

---

## ANSWER KEY 4.G.A.1
1. b. ray
2. Student should draw a right, obtuse, and acute angle

Right angle:

Obtuse angle:

Acute angle:

3. a. parallel
   b. perpendicular
   c. intersecting
4. a. right angle (forms a right angle, which equals 90º)
   b. obtuse angle (greater than 90 º)
   c. acute angle (less than 90º)
   d. straight line (180º)
The student should trace either the top and bottom (horizontal) lines of the rectangle or the two sides (vertical lines) of the rectangle.

## ANSWER KEY 4.G.A.2
1. Yes, there are 2 sets of parallel lines.
2. Perpendicular
3. All the angles are right angles.
4. No, a rectangle is not a square. Like a rectangle, all four angles of a square are 90º; however, all 4 sides of a square are congruent, while only the rectangle's opposite sides are congruent.
5. b

## ANSWER KEY 4.G.A.3
1. The following letters should be circled:
A B C D E H I K M O T U V W X Y
2.

3. a. 5  b. 1  c. 2
4. A circle has an unlimited number of lines of symmetry because there are an infinite number of lines that can be drawn through the center of a circle.
5. Yes. It can be folded so that the two parts of the figure match (congruent).
6. No. Equilateral triangles have 3 lines of symmetry.